AUTHORITY, LIBERTY AND FUNCTION
IN THE LIGHT OF THE WAR

I0103769

AUTHORITY, LIBERTY AND FUNCTION *in the* LIGHT OF THE WAR

A CRITIQUE OF AUTHORITY AND LIBERTY AS THE FOUNDATIONS OF THE MODERN STATE AND AN ATTEMPT TO BASE SO-CIETIES ON THE PRINCIPLE OF FUNCTION

BY

RAMIRO DE MAEZTU

LONDON : GEORGE ALLEN & UNWIN LTD.
RUSKIN HOUSE   40 MUSEUM STREET, W.C.
NEW YORK : THE MACMILLAN COMPANY

First published in 1916

(All rights reserved)

PREFACE

THE contents of this book have appeared between March 1915 and June 1916 in the *New Age*. But the volume is not merely a collection of articles, for most of them were written with a view to the place they would occupy in the completed work, and every chapter has been revised. I owe to the *New Age* and its editor, Mr. A. R. Orage, the idea of the Guilds; to M. Léon Duguit that of objective rights; to Mr. G. E. Moore that of objective good; to Herr Edmond Husserl that of objective logic; and to Mr. T. E. Hulme the acknowledgment of the political and social transcendency of the doctrine of original sin. I wish to express my thanks to all, and also to Mr. J. M. Kennedy, who has shared with me the labour of giving my thoughts this English setting, and to Messrs. A. R. Orage and Rowland Kenney for their numerous corrections.

CONTENTS

AUTHORITY AND POWER

LIBERTY AND HAPPINESS

CONTENTS

8

FUNCTION AND VALUES

AUTHORITY AND POWER

AUTHORITY, LIBERTY & FUNCTION
IN THE LIGHT OF THE WAR

THE GERMAN HERESY

I

The Man of the Renaissance

It has been said that the central ideas of the
Middle Ages consisted in looking upon the world
as a vale of tears, and upon man as " I, a sinner."
That is why the Middle Ages have been accused
of darkening the world and diminishing man, as
if their judgments of both were not recognitions
of two facts, but the expressions of a malignant
and anti-human will. But that the world is a vale
of tears, and that man is " I, a sinner," are not
judgments characteristic of a given period of
humanity. They must have been thought by men
of all ages in consequence of that which really
distinguishes man from all other beings on earth :
the ideal of perfection in his soul. When this
ideal of perfection is applied to the region of the
senses, the world must appear to us as a vale of
tears ; when it is applied to the moral plane man
has to be depicted as " I, a sinner." Desire has
nothing to do with these judgments. They are
the judgments of experience. They are facts.
There may come a day when God will deprive

man—to give it to other animals ; perhaps to the frogs—of this privilege, at once his glory and his tragedy, of being the only living thing which can conceive perfection ; but so long as he does conceive it he is bound to say, when he looks outward with impartial eyes : " This world is a vale of tears," and when he looks inwards : " I am a sinner."

The characteristic of the Middle Ages is not the acknowledgment of these two eternal and inevitable facts ; but the imaginative way in which they reacted against them. The men who lived in Europe between the eighth and the twelfth centuries may be compared to those lonely children who create a playmate with their imagination and carry on long talks with him, believe that they hear his replies, and live so enwrapped in their dreams that they scarcely notice either their solitude or the world surrounding them. All these things of reality, which now imprison us with thick and cruel walls, were at that time nothing more than a subtle veil— which imagination easily tore asunder so as to contemplate the choirs of seraphim and cherubim around the Lord. The air was filled with benevolent angels and memories of saints. Men could speak daily with their guardian angels. It is also true that the air was saturated with unholy legions. The gods of Paganism, Jupiter, Minerva, Venus, Mars, Pluto, Mercury, Diana, Bacchus and their *daimones*, were devils and she-devils who never ceased from tempting men into sin, but the sign of the Cross, or a few drops of holy water, or the name of Mary, was enough to put the arch-fiend to flight. In spite of this exaltation, terrorism was unknown. Although the torments of hell were hard, good Christians believed themselves to be free of them. The Christ they adored was the sweet Good Shepherd, who adorns the chapels of the Catacombs.

The melancholy and terrible image of Christ does not become popular until towards the twelfth century. There was no religious persecution. The Inquisition was not established until the thirteenth century. There was no belief in witches. The conception of the witch became clear only during the twelfth century. It is an error to attribute to the Christian Middle Ages the terrifying superstitions of the Cabala, an invention of unorthodox Jews ; alchemy, an Arab invention ; and astrology, which was at its height in the fifteenth century, in the very middle of the Renaissance. Life in the Middle Ages was not a nightmare, but a dream —an amorous dream of heaven.

In the twelfth century came the awakening. It has been said that the cause of this awakening was the natural development of the human mind. But I do not believe in the natural development of the human mind, and I shall not believe in such a thing until it is proved to me that men transmit arts and letters to their children. So long as it is not proved to me that heredity extends to the kingdom of the spirit, I shall persist in attributing changes in human mentality to external and historical events. In my judgment the awakening of Europe in the twelfth century was due to a cause analogous to that which is bringing about the awakening of England in the twentieth. That cause was war. While the air of Europe was being filled with angels and saints and devils, while the schoolmen elaborated complicated theologies, and while the peoples constructed systems of government in which the powers of the Emperor and the Pope, the aristocracy and the hierarchy, the guilds of the towns, the lords of the lands, and the religious orders were delicately balanced one against another, the Arabic Empire was being

established in Asia, in Africa, and in Spain—a
military, despotic, and unitary Empire, with a lonely
God in heaven and Mahomet's scimitar on earth.
The advance of the Mohammedans led to the wars
of Spain, of Sicily, and the Crusades. In these
wars Europeans had to face a different world. Wars
were followed by truces, in which began the peaceful
intercourse of ideas and products. Through Palermo
and Toledo a knowledge of Arab science and
philosophy filtered into Europe. Through Venice
and her spice and slave-trade were discovered the
sea routes to the East. The soldiers of the Fourth
Crusade made the schoolmen of Paris interested in
the language and literature of Greece.

Confronted with the imperious will of the Semitic
peoples, the mind of Europe awoke from its dream.
This awakening we call the Renaissance. In this
awakening man discovers gunpowder, printing, and
the sea-routes to the East and West Indies. At
the same time he unearths the manuscripts of
antiquity, and publishes the works of Plato, Aristotle,
Virgil, Seneca, and a score of other authors,
displaying magnificent vistas hitherto unknown. He
tries to harmonize the ideas of the ancients with
his own, and in this attempt he produces the
basis of modern civilization. The fruits of the
Renaissance may be described by the headings of
the chapters in Burckhardt's book : " Development
of the Individual," " Revival of Antiquity," " Discovery of the World and of Man." These fruits
are undoubtedly good, and the sphere of the good
is much larger than that of morality. For every
good work of art, even if immoral, is good, since
it is æsthetically good, though it would be better
if it were, besides, good in its moral content.
Every new and true thought, like every geographical
discovery, increases the number of good things,

in the same way as a good action does. Every good work of art or science is, as well, a good action. And since the Renaissance was a great period of art, of thought, and of economic activity, it is implied that it was also an epoch which considerably increased the number of good things.

But there is in the nature of man the capacity to fool himself with the most dangerous of fooleries. When a man does a good thing, and clearly realizes that the thing is good, if he forgets for a moment that he, the author of the good thing, does not cease on its account to be a sinner, he will easily fall into the temptation of believing himself to be good. "My work is good, therefore I am good." Such is the sophism of pride, the gravest of all the motives of sin that afflict mankind. For the causes of sin are two, and two only: lust and pride. Lust—immoderate appetite—comes from the animal side of our nature. Pride, on the other hand, comes from our rational side. It comes from above, not from below. It begins in a theory, a reasoning: "My work is good, therefore I am good." When the first of these two clauses is false, when the work is not good, or a man has not done a good work, pride is relatively harmless, for it is pure vanity. But when the work is really good the lever of pride finds in the goodness of the work the point of support it requires to move the world in the direction of evil. I need hardly say that the theory of pride is false. We know the lives of some of the men who performed the best actions recorded in history. Those lives show us that the men were not good, though their works were. If you know artists and intellectuals, you know also that they are not good men. Nor were the geniuses any better. And the saints, who, overcoming their nature, lived, on the whole, saintly lives, were only sinners. What makes a saint a saint is that he hardly ever loses the consciousness of being a sinner. And the sin of the devil is pride. The devil is the devil because he believes himself to be good.

This was the sin of the men of the Renaissance. When the Mantuan spoke in the fifteenth century on the seven monsters, he described the Humanists in the chapter entitled "Superbia." The Humanists were the discoverers and the dispensers of fame. As poets and historians they judged of the glory of others. They enjoyed an extended reputation throughout Italy. The ceremony of the coronation of the poets was the symbol to which tended "lo gran disio dell' eccellenza." And this desire for glory was so intense throughout Italy, that it was possible for a man to take away, without being punished, the lamps from the altar of the crucifix and place them on the grave of a famous man, saying, "Take them; you are more worthy of them than the other" (the Crucified). Towards the end of the sixteenth century the Italian people were as disgusted with the vanity, the egotism, and the self-idolatry of the Humanists as with their immoral habits. But by then the Humanist idea had spread all over Europe. The Humanist idea at that time meant the study of the ancient classics with the aim of finding in human history, as opposed to sacred history, the models with which to inspire the education of the coming generations. After that the Humanists were attacked on account of their exclusive preference for the study of Latin and Greek. In opposition to the Humanists, the "Philanthropists" of the eighteenth and nineteenth centuries upheld the study of modern science. But, at the bottom, both Humanists and Philanthropists shared the same ideas: that nothing human should be alien to them, that all human religions and beliefs have contributed to the progress of man, and that man is the spiritual centre of the world. " All things are for men, but men are for one another." " Man is an end," Goethe used to say. " Respect humanity in thy person and in that of others, not as a means, but as an end," was Kant's formula.

This formulation of ethics is obviously false. An action is not good through being altruistic or humane ; nor evil through being egoistic or inhumane. The other, the neighbour, is as much a sinner as I am. There is not the slightest reason why I should sacrifice myself for the benefit of a friend who asks me for money, if I know he is going to play with his money at Monte Carlo. A single man—Jesus on the Cross or Socrates drinking his hemlock—may be right against the whole world. Because Humanist ethics was false, its consequences had to be bad. And they were bad. Men lost through it the consciousness of living in sin. And with the consciousness of living in sin disappeared the spiritual rein which checked their evil impulses. The man who follows the Renaissance has lost the spiritual check because he does not feel himself to be a sinner. He is the man of Shakespeare—Othello, Macbeth, Falstaff, Romeo, Hamlet. Nothing restrains him. He is a law unto himself, to use the happy expression of St. Paul. Precisely because he believes only in himself he has even ceased to be a man ; he has become the slave of his own passions.

This pride of man, which brings about his ruin, is aggravated when Descartes proclaims that the universe of things is contained in the universe of the human mind, that sciences consist of the knowledge of the mind, that everything rises from reason,

2

and that methodic doubt on all things only disappears with the formula : " *Cogito, ergo sum* " (" I think, therefore I am "). The Cartesian doubt is certainly the beginning of wisdom. I do not know what I know ; I am not sure of what I know ; but I am sure that I think.' Up to this point Descartes is right. But to think is to think of something. This something is something different from the thought itself. Therefore, to think is to be sure of something objective of which we are thinking, and which is indicated by the thought. Uncertainty affects only the particular something of which we are thinking. The something, in general, is given to us as immediately as thought itself. This objective something, constituted by things, is what guarantees the certainty of our thought, which without this something could be nothing more than a pure dream. The truth lies not in the thought or in the things, but only in their relation. It may be said that a thought is true when it is valid for the things. The centre of truth, therefore, is not in man ; but in an intermediate point between men and things. But Descartes has subjectivized it. After Descartes, men could say proudly : " My thought is the measure of things."

And when man ceased to have any other rein than himself, the result was not the unity of all men—for men cannot unite immediately among one another ; they unite in things, in common values—but the struggle of man against man, " and such a war, as is of every man against every man." When Hobbes describes " The Natural Condition of Mankind as Concerning their Felicity and their Misery," he has in mind, as he could not help having, the man of his own seventeenth century. And it is with this man before his eyes that he writes : —

" So that in the nature of man, we find three principal causes of quarrel. First, competition ; secondly, diffidence ; thirdly, glory. The first, maketh men invade for gain ; the second, for safety ; and the third, for reputation. . . . To this war of every man, against every man, this also is consequent ; that nothing can be unjust. The notions of right and wrong, justice and injustice, have there no place. Where there is no common power, there is no law ; where no law, no injustice. Force and fraud are in war the two cardinal virtues."

Frightful words, these. Man is depicted as a beast of prey let loose upon the world. This beast has to be bound. From this practical necessity there arises in the mind of Hobbes and in the history of Europe the modern State with its centralized powers: the State as a necessity. But the Germans have gone a step further: they have converted the necessity into a good ; they have invented the State as the good. And this is the German heresy.

II

THE STATE AS NECESSITY.

THE modern State arises from the necessity of ordering social life in a stable way. The classic theories of the State confirm this assertion. We know how Hobbes founds this institution. In the state of nature, where men fight with one another " for gain," " for security," and " for reputation " —and this is a war " of every man against every man," in which there is no law, no " notions of right and wrong," but only " force " and " fraud " —there arises in men the wish for order. " The

passions that incline men to peace are fear of
death ; desire of such things as are necessary to
commodious living ; and a hope by their industry
of obtaining them." On these passions Hobbes
builds his State. Its only mission is the performance of covenants. In order that covenants may
be performed, there is need of a supreme authority
which shall cause them to be performed. This
authority does not need to care whether the
contracts are just or unjust ; for " the definition
of ' injustice ' is no other than ' the not performance of covenant.' " Here it is obvious that Hobbes
has no illusions as to the morality of the State.
His State is not founded on morality, but on
necessity in the sense of convenience.

Against Hobbes, who denies the natural goodness of man, rises Rousseau, who asserts it. Hence
a different conception of society. Hobbes upholds
the utility of all the " artificial " elements of social
life: civilization, the sovereign, the juridical fiction
of personality. Rousseau, instead, wishes man to
maintain his nature as far as possible within social
life. While Hobbes wishes the peoples to obey
the princes, Rousseau tells them that they are the
princes: " Power can be transmitted, but not will."
Rousseau's problem is that of: " Finding a form
of association which defends and protects with all
the common force the person and property of every
associate, and by which each one, uniting himself
to all, nevertheless obeys only himself, and remains
as free as before." It is here a question of found-
ing the State to protect the person and property of
every man. This aim is as purely utilitarian as that
of Hobbes. Rousseau himself admits it: " I suppose that men have now arrived at that point at
which the obstacles which prevent them from maintaining themselves in a state of nature overcome

through their resistance the powers that every individual can employ to keep himself in his natural state." Rousseau's solution is the formula of his Social Contract: " Each one of us puts in common his person and all his power under the supreme direction of the general will ; and we then receive each member as an indivisible part of the whole."

Neither Hobbes nor Rousseau has any illusions as to the aims of the State. All that they ask from it is that it shall " guarantee the covenants," or that it shall " fulfil the common will," that it shall " impose peace," or that it shall " cause persons and property to be respected." In spite of the modesty of this aim, both Hobbes and Rousseau wish the State to assume the supreme, unique, and absolute power. " Sovereignty is indivisible," says Rousseau. " The social pact gives to the body politic absolute sovereignty over all its subjects." " When the prince says to the citizen, ' It suits the State that you should die,' the citizen ought to die ; for it is only on this condition that he has lived in security until then, and his life is not only a benefit from Nature, but a conditional gift of the State." If a republican and a democrat like Rousseau uses language of this kind, we cannot hope that Hobbes, the theorist of absolute monarchy, should haggle over the powers of the State. " The sovereign power, whether placed in one man, as in monarchy, or in one assembly of men, as in popular and aristocratical commonwealths, is as great as possibly men can be imagined to make it." To create a power capable of defending men from the invasion of foreigners, and from mutual injury, a man or an assembly of men must be nominated to whom all powers shall be entrusted, " and therein to submit their wills, every one to his will, and their judgments, to his judgment." " This is the generation of that great ' leviathan,' or rather, to speak more reverently, of that ' mortal God,' to which we owe under the ' immortal God ' our peace and defence."

All the political theories of the modern epoch express the tendency to conceive the State as a unity of power and as the category of all organized society. I have quoted Hobbes and Rousseau ; I could also have leaned upon Bodin and Grotius. Up to the emergence of the syndicalist theory,—I do not speak of anarchistic and individualistic theories, precisely because they are anarchistic and individualistic—nobody has conceived the possibility of an ordered society not based on this unity of power called the State, and which, in fact, is characteristic of modern societies. In this way the State is promoted to the rank of a category, an inevitable institution. But when the societies of the Middle Ages are studied, it is seen that they lacked exactly, this unity of power which characterizes the modern State. A double dualism prevailed in them ; the king and the people ; the spiritual and the temporal powers. And since the State is defined as the unity of power, and as the Middle Ages were characterized by the multiplicity of supreme powers, it has to be said that in the Middle Ages there was no State, which is either a modern invention or a resurrection of the political systems of paganism. The theorists of the State have accentuated the necessity of unifying all social powers in it, because they could not see any other alternative to the absolutism of the State than disorder. Hobbes says: " And though of so unlimited power men may fancy many evil consequences, yet the consequences of the want of it, which is perpetual war of every man against his neighbour, are much worse." The Middle Ages show us that this alternative of Hobbes was false. In the societies that built the Gothic churches, founded the universities, and organized the Guilds, man was certainly not more aggressive towards man than he is in modern times, in which all powers are unified in the State.

The dilemma which would make us choose between the State and anarchy is false. There is another alternative: that of the plurality and the balance of powers, not merely within the nation but in the family of nations. This balance of powers is difficult to reach and preserve, because every one of the powers inevitably aspires to hegemony. The balance is maintained only at the price of eternal vigilance. But have we not to pay the same price for friendship, for health, for talent, and for all the goods of life, if we wish to prolong their duration beyond the limits of their own spontaneity? If one thinks that the unification of social powers in the State makes it possible for the totality of those powers to be wasted in a war, or in a series of wars, such as those which exhausted, in the sixteenth century, the rich vitality of the Spanish people, is it not, after all, preferable to order our social life in a plurality of powers carefully balanced? Why did this thought escape the foresight of Machiavelli, Bodin, Grotius, Hobbes, Rousseau, and the other theorists of the modern State?

It did not occur to them because the stability of the societies of the Middle Ages was based precisely upon that of their Corporations, and these were dissolving, apparently for ever, before the very eyes of the theorists of the State. They were not merely dissolving materially; morally they were already dissolved. They were dissolved by the " great " discovery of human personality which we owe to the Renaissance. When men believed that their highest duties consisted, not in serving the Corporation to which they belonged, but in developing their own personality, the clergyman left the Church to become a humanist, a heretic, or the minister of a king ; the landlords neglected the duties which had come down to them with their property, and began to see in their estates only, the source of the revenues they needed to live at Court, in the capital, or in foreign countries ; their very tenants aided the cupidity of the lords by becoming their relentless agents ; the masters gave up the Guilds to turn into employers, and to exploit their workmen with full freedom in the new free towns. As individualism had destroyed the Corporations, and the theorists of the State could not visualize the possibility of resurrecting them, they conceived the thought of unifying all powers as the only means of saving society from the anarchy of the war of every man against every man. And it was not only in theory, but also in the practical world, that the Leviathan of the State became indispensable.

Modern jurists frequently speak of the atomization of the State in the Middle Ages. In reality it was not atomic. The truth is that the Middle Ages were atomized in the centuries that followed them. The characteristic fact of European societies between the fifteenth and nineteenth centuries was that the Corporations were abandoned by their most energetic members. And from this dissolution of the corporate life has arisen the modern unitary State, as an historic and temporal necessity, but not as an eternal necessity ; not as a category of social life. But if the State is not a category, if it is purely an historic institution which arises at the bidding of a momentary necessity, it runs the risk of vanishing from history with the necessity which has called it into existence. And that, in fact, was what had occurred in the mentality of thinkers and was on the point of happening in reality. When the war of 1914 broke out the institution of the State was on the point of disappearing from among the peoples of Western Europe. The thinkers, at least, had already ceased to believe in the necessity for it. It was defended only by the politicians; but there did not remain a single public man who enjoyed the confidence placed in his predecessors. This was not the fault of the men. Personally, they may have been as clever and good then as were the statesmen of old. But we called them politicians and not statesmen, for we no longer believed in the State.

In this sense we may interpret the German aggression as the last effort made in defence of the State. The Germany of 1914 still believed in the State. Firm in this faith, she found herself in a situation analogous to that of Spain, who, in the sixteenth century, realized her religious unity at the very moment in which the rest of Europe lost it. And as Spain then threw herself on Europe to impose religious unity, so Germany threw herself on Europe to impose the unity of the State. Strengthened in their State religion, the Germans replied: "We" to Nietzsche's question: "Wer soll der Erde Herr sein?" ("Who shall be master of the world?") Already in 1913 Ernst Horneffer eloquently announced that the next war "will be fought on the organized power of the whole earthly globe." And he promised victory to the Germans on the ground that they themselves had created their own God, the State, with the words of Schiller:—

> Rühmend darf's der Deutsche sagen . . .
> Selbst erschuf er sich den Wert.
> (Proudly may the German say . . . he has
>   created his own value.)

Why did Europeans of the Western nations cease to believe in the State? Why did the Germans go on believing in it? Because the belief of the Westerners in the State was based exclusively on the supposition that the unification of all the powers was necessary for the ordering of social life. The history of the nineteenth century, has shown the falsity of this belief. The last hundred years marked in all countries the beginning of the dissolution of the State and of the resurrection of corporate life. In the early decades of the last century, when the States were abolishing the last vestiges of the Corporations, the workmen were beginning to revive them, urged on by the necessity of defending themselves against the cupidity of capitalism. At the end of their struggles the Trade Unions do not seem to us to be merely associations for the defence of working-class interests, but institutions of order and discipline. By their growth alone they have revealed to us the possibility of a social order without the need of a sole power. If only the methods of the Trade Unions be extended to all classes in social life, organized with respect to their functions, and the legitimacy of even a capitalist class is recognized—so long as it fulfils a necessary function, such as that of collecting the savings of one generation in order to prepare for the work of the next, and only in so far as it fulfils this function—then the need for a unitarian State will automatically disappear. In the face of this growth of syndicalism in every direction, revolutionary as well as reactionary, it is no longer venturesome to assert that the State is dead.

Why, then, do the Germans continue to believe in it? Because in Germany the State has not been conceived purely as a necessity, but as a good in itself. There are philosophical schools who treat it as *the* good. So long as the State is considered merely as a necessity, it will no longer be defended when facts prove that it has ceased to be necessary. But if it is defended as a good or a duty, or as the duty and the good, it will be defended even after it has ceased to be necessary. And this is what has happened in Germany. There the corporate life is as intense as in Great Britain, and more intense than in France. That ought to prove to the Germans that the State, in the sense of the unity of power, is no longer necessary. There are Germans who see this. In the Left of German Socialism there are men who are not unfamiliar with the meaning of syndicalism. But in Germany the State is not only a political invention, but an ethical idea.

III

THE STATE AS THE GOOD.

THE German theory of the State consists substantially in asserting that when an organ of the State carries out an action in the service of the State that action is necessarily good. According to this theory the State is the good ; and not only the good thing, but the good agent. It is at once the subject and the object of the ethical life—the kisser, the kiss, and the kissed ; the lover, the love, and the beloved. The State that wills itself is, according to these German theories, the supreme formula of moral life. "The State as self-consciousness," says Cohen, " is the unity of the subject and the object in the will."

This theory is not upheld in Germany by the Conservative parties alone, but also by the Demo-

cratic parties. Othmar Spann is an Imperialist, a
partisan of the war, and at the same time one of
the most brilliant spirits of the new generation.
If you read the book which he dedicated in 1913
(mark the date) to the :' Sociology and Philosophy.
of War," you will find these words: :" In the sacrifice of war life is not sacrificed to the State as a
means of life, but to the State as the bearer of
life itself. Life is sacrificed to itself ; to its own
higher and last ends. Those sacrifices which we
bring to life we ought to bring also to the State."
And how could it be otherwise when, according to
this philosophy, the State is the highest and last
end of life ?

But Hermann Cohen is not a " vitalist " or an
Imperialist or a Nationalist ; but such a good
Liberal and Socialist and Pacifist that when the
Bismarck anniversary was celebrated he used to have
the civic courage to say to his pupils at the University of Marburg : :" This is a sad day for the history
of Germany." Nevertheless, Cohen's ethics, too,
is the ethics of the State. Cohen's State is not
exclusively the national or imperial State that we
know. It is rather the union of the States of
humanity, wherein is guaranteed that :" eternal
peace " which, according to Kant, is the eternal
orientation of morality. But that does not diminish,
in Cohen's philosophy, the ethical value of the
present or empirical State. :" Its value does not
consist in its actual reality, but in being a directive
concept of ethical self-consciousness." The State
comes first—before the family, before the nation,
before religion. In the case of a conflict between
the nation and the State, as in nations which have
lost their State—like the Jews and the Poles—love
is owed to the lost State, but obedience and
dependence to the actual State. The State of

" eternal peace " is reached only through the development of the actual State: " The direction for the formation of a genuine self-consciousness of the ethic personality consists, for us, in the submerging of one's own ego in the plenitudes and in the energies of the directions and moral activities which run together in the unity of the State."

But whence does Cohen deduce this supreme excellence of the State? Simply from the fact that the State represents in the social life the concept of " totality," to which all particularities must be submitted. Ethics, according to Cohen, deals with the co-relation between the individual and the totality. The totality, from which is derived the concept of man, the object of ethics, cannot be given by the individual or the race or the Church, but by the State ; for the States can be united in one State which comprises the whole of humanity, and the Churches cannot. Man is not what he believes himself to be in the sensual feeling of himself. It is only in the State that he becomes a man. Morality is not self-evident in the individual, but in the totality of Universal History, and it is the State which presents to us the correspondence of all the problems in the totality. The unity of man is not an actual reality, but a juridical fiction, a juridical concept. The State is the model concept which serves to form the concept of man.

These reasonings are confused, and I do not ask the general reader to understand them. To be able to grasp them requires a certain familiarity with the idealistic philosophy, which says that there exists in man a kind of pure will—the ethical will, which is pure because it does not will the things, but wills the purity ; or, what amounts to the same thing, it wills itself. This pure will is the State.

But why the State? In answering this question the astounding simplicity which underlies the immense complexity of idealistic terminology becomes self-evident. Cohen replies that in the individual it is impossible to separate the pure will from the empiric will, because man is not only will, but also instinct. To the State, on the other hand, we attribute will ; but it is not possible to attribute to it instinct. In the State there is will, but no instinct. Hence, the will of the State is the pure will.

It is true that Cohen's philosophy is not the predominant philosophy in Germany. But, although the reader may be surprised at the statement, it is not predominant precisely on account of its individualism. Cohen assumes that when two individuals enter into a contract there arises a third subject, the contract itself, whose will is pure, because it is not mixed with instinct. This contract, when it has a social character, is the State. And though the will of the State is supreme, and must prevail over the individuals, it still arises from the individuals ; from the social side of the individuals. This is what the predominant theory in Germany does not admit ; for it continues to believe, with Hegel, that in the beginning was the social ; that the social is an autonomous category—which is true ; that it is a value in itself—which is also true ; that it cannot be reduced to any anterior fact— which is also true ; and that the social is the State —an assertion which is no longer true ; for the State is only one among many other products of the social, and may disappear from the face of the earth without society disappearing with it.

This priority of the State is not chronological. Hegel asserts that the social is historically anterior to the State. What Hegel says is that the State is the highest expression and the organ of social morality ; that it is in the State that man realizes his moral being and his free will ; that it is the State which maintains the personality of man, protecting his welfare and withdrawing him from his selfishness. For the individual, " whose tendency is to convert himself into a centre of his own," needs a superior power which shall carry him back " into the life of the universal substance." At the present time Hegel's philosophy may perhaps be regarded as dead. But his theory of the State has never ceased to prevail in Germany. And this theory is characteristically German, of the Germany of the nineteenth century. It has been upheld in other countries, too. In England it has been maintained to a certain extent by Green, Bosanquet, and Bradley ; but the influence of these men has never passed beyond the bounds of academic circles.

The political history of Germany is not alone the cause of this German conception of the State. German politics have made its triumph possible. The fact that Prussia is a unitary State of implacable military and bureaucratic character is explained by its geographical position and by the epoch in which it was constituted. Placed in the middle of the Continent, among the greatest military Powers of Europe, it could not assert its independence except by the most ferocious discipline and the most systematized unity. If it had been a nation governed by different internal powers, as Poland, with a similar geographical position, was governed by bishops and Jesuits, noblemen and kings, it would have run the risk of suffering the same fate. History explains the political régime of Prussia without its being necessary to attribute

it to the despotism of its monarchs, the innate
discipline of the Prussians, or a lack of liberal
spirit in the Germanic race.

History may explain to us also that a man like
Kant, in spite of his admiration for Rousseau and
for the French Revolution, could preach to the
people, in his " Metaphysic of Customs," unconditional obedience to the authorities, with a rigour
that would have pleased even Hobbes himself.
When Kant says that we must obey the authorities
who have power over us, " without asking who has
given them the right to command us," his advice
is not based on the idea that the absolute power of
the authorities is good in itself, but on the fact that
it is necessary that the supreme power shall determine what is right and what is not right.   And
this necessity of the absolute power of the State,
although based by Kant " a priori on the idea of
a constitution of the State in general," may also
be interpreted as a necessity originated in the imperfection of human nature.   Kant draws a radical
distinction between ethical legislation, in which duty
is the only stimulus of the action, and juridical
legislation, in which the action is determined by
stimuli, such as the fear of punishment, distinct
from the idea of duty.   Here the necessity of law
is clearly based upon the imperfection of human
nature.   And this is a permanent and philosophic
reason and not an historical one.   But when Kant
tells us that we must obey whoever has power over
us, although it may be a usurped or illegitimate
power, it is impossible to find any other reason for
his advice than an historical one ; the convenience
or necessity of maintaining at all costs, at a given
moment, the coherence of a particular society.   For
my part I am inclined to believe that what makes
Kant the Liberal an unconditional subject of the

King of Prussia is the fact that he lived towards the end of the eighteenth century in Koenigsberg, not very far from the Russian frontier.

In Kant the unitary State is nothing more than a necessity, as it is in Hobbes and Rousseau. How does it come to be turned into a good? In our reply we can no longer be guided by the political history of Germany, but by the history of the ideology of her thinkers. If Kant rigidly separates the moral world—in which actions are autonomous, because they only receive a stimulus from the idea of duty —from the legal world, in which actions are heteronomous, because they are affected by the coercive power of the State, how does Germany come to identify the State with the good? Kant himself is responsible for this confusion, not in his doctrine of the State, but in his ethics. Kant's ethics is subjectivist, in the sense that it derives the goodness of the actions from the goodness of the agent. If an action is good, that must be due to the goodness of the agent carrying it out. This consequence is unacceptable, because it contradicts the certain fact that men who are not good nevertheless carry out good actions. This consequence is only an application to the moral world of the logical idealism that made Kant believe that an exact knowledge is impossible unless it is thought by a pure-thinking being. But the fact is that Kant assumes the existence of an agent (substance or function) in the human soul which carries out good actions. This agent is Practical Reason. Practical Reason is not, however, the State. But it is trans-individual and super-individual.

What is Practical Reason? Fichte interprets Kant by saying that it is the Ego. Fichte's Ego is absolute and comprises everything—the external world as well as the internal. Kant has opened the way

3

to this identity of the external and the internal with the identity which he establishes between " the conditions of the possibility of experience " and " the conditions of the possibility of the objects of the experience." This identity, which in Kant is relative, is made absolute by Fichte, who calls it Ego— an Ego which lets itself be determined by the non-Ego when the problem is logical or of knowledge, but which determines the non-Ego when the problem is ethical or of action. This is equivalent to saying that the Ego of Fichte determines everything ; for, if it allows itself to be determined by the non-Ego in logic in order to study. Nature, it is the Ego itself which consents to it. For moral life to be possible, the Ego begins by postulating a matter of the action, and in this way it creates Nature ; but at the same time it must assert itself as form. The practical Ego is at once the matter and form of the action. This Ego is not yet the State. Fichte, like Kant, is not a philosopher of the State but a philosopher of freedom. But while Kant reflected in Koenigsberg at a certain distance from the Cossacks, Fichte pronounced some of his " Discourses to the German Nation " as he heard from his classroom the rattling of the sabres of the French patrols as they marched along the streets. Nevertheless, Fichte's Ego is not yet the State, although his predication consists in advising the Germans to give themselves up to the State as a matter of duty. But the principles of the separation made by Kant between the moral and legal life have disappeared in Fichte. His Ego comprises both the autonomous and heteronomous actions. The barriers have fallen : when Hegel arises the road is quite clear.

IV

HEGEL AND THE STATE.

HEGEL is spoken of as a philosopher. Hegel is, in truth, the greatest heresiarch the world has produced since the days of Arius and Mahomet. His philosophy is a religion in which unitarianism and trinitarianism are fused into one. He is a unitarian in his pantheistic proposition: " All is one and the same." He is a trinitarian in so far as he discovers three moments in this great unity which is at once the world and God : the moment of position, that of negation, and that of the synthesis of position and negation. His all, which is " one and the same," proceeds by triads. This all, the Absolute, spirit and not matter, is of a dialectical nature, and is subject to perpetual becoming and eternal flux. " Gott ist in Werden " (God becomes). And he says that as if he had authority for knowing it. There was never an agnostic so convinced as Hegel of having penetrated into the mysteries of the Divine Essence. Already when he began to study theology in the University of Tübingen his fellow-students called him " *der alte Mann* " (" the old man "). And this trembling respect is easily explained. Hegel's central position is blasphemous and unscientific. The spirit of truth has not been given to man to invent the world but to discover it. But no man ever made a greater attempt to draw the universe from his own head. And, just as Wagner's enemies never denied his wealth of exquisite phrases, neither can Hegel's enemies deny that no other man, with the exception of St. Paul and Pascal, has expressed the drama of human destinies in a greater number of lapidary sentences.

Everything in the world is becoming, says Hegel. Everywhere the Being is found surrounded by the No More, the Not Yet, and the Not Quite. Why? Because the Being is Becoming, Evolution. Hegel's Absolute is not a dead thing, or a unity in repose, like that of Schelling : " A night in which all cows are black " ; but life, spirit, development, and, at the same time, reason or idea. The idea has three moments : that of position, in itself and for itself, which is dealt with by Logic ; that of negation, in which the idea comes out of itself to be in something else (Nature) which is studied in Natural Philosophy ; and that of the synthesis, in which the idea comes back to itself after having been in something else ; and this is dealt with by the Philosophy of the Spirit. With that we have sketched the total triad of Hegel's system.

The logical moment is decomposed into another triad : (1) the pure being, without content ; (2) the essence, in which the being seems reflected in itself ; and (3) the concept, in which the particular appears as the phenomenon of the universal. The natural moment, in which the idea comes out of itself, has another three moments : (1) pure externality (space, time, movement, gravitation) ; (2) the externality animates itself into energy (cohesion, electricity, magnetism, chemical affinities) ; and (3) the animation converts itself into individual shapes and into life—stones, plants, and animals. With that we pass to the spiritual moment in which the idea comes back to itself. First, it asserts itself in man (anthropology, phenomenology, and psychology) ; then it objectivises itself in action (law, morality, and " Sittlichkeit "—family, civil society, and State) ; and, finally, the spirit makes itself absolute in art, religion, and philosophy.

This last absolute moment does not interest us.

What does interest us is that the objective spirit of Hegel begins in the moment of Law and culminates in the moment of the State. Subjective morality is nothing autonomous for Hegel, but a point of transit between legality and the State. The objective spirit is realized in the State. The individual must worship in the State the synthesis of the earthly and the heavenly. To the State, on the other hand, the destiny of the individual is indifferent. Its authority is unconditional. It is true that the State ought to be an organization of freedom ; but what is important for Hegel is the institution of hereditary monarchy, for there must be somebody " to dot the i's." In his " Philosophy of Law " he prints in large type the famous phrase : " What is rational is real ; what is real is rational." His State, therefore, is the concrete State constituted by the monarchy and the bureaucracy of Prussia. Plato's " aristoi " are the bureaucrats of Prussia. And this State of Hegel is above all idea of contract. " None of the citizens belongs to himself, for they all belong to the State." It is, again, above all international morality, for " War shows the omnipotence of the State in its individuality," and " everything real is rational."

When Hegel published his " Philosophy of Law " in 1821 he had witnessed the national reaction against Napoleon in the War of Liberation (1812) ; he had seen that the hold which the national State had on men's minds could not be explained by any idea of contract, and Hegel attributes it to the real and personal existence of the nation and the State, instead of attributing it, as he ought to have done, to the enthusiasm which every just cause excites in noble spirits aware of its justice. In 1818 he succeeded Fichte in the Chair of Philosophy in Berlin University. Philosophy was then Germany's

favourite science. It had then the same fascination for men's minds as had religion in periods
of theological crises. It was the religion of the
day. A few years before there were forty teachers
at the University of Jena, and sixteen of them
lectured on philosophy. At the end of the second
decade of the nineteenth century Hegel was the
foremost intellectual figure of Germany. The ·
Minister von Altenstein realized that Hegel's philosophy, precisely because it raised the State to the
category of a divinity, suited the interests of the
Government, and he placed Hegelians in the philosophical Chairs of the Prussian Universities. Then
the Hegelians were divided into Centre, Left, and
Right. But Hegel's philosophy of law is still
triumphant. Whether the State is considered as
an " organism," as an " organ," as a " personality," as " the organic manifestation of a nation "
(Savigny), as the " realization of morality " (Tredelenburg), as an " organization of social compulsion " (Ihering), or as the " form of the instinct
for order " (Rumelin) : in every definition of the
State by a German author one finds involved a
positive moral valuation, as if the concept of the
good were comprised in that of the State. And the
hundred thousand schoolmasters in the German
schools insist more on showing that goodness is
immanent in the State than in trying to define what
the State is.   ·

Only in the course of the last few years, and
then in consequence of the criticism of the Frenchman Duguit, have a few specialists, such as Loening,
discovered that the State is nothing but the juridical
relation between rulers and ruled. Thus the State
ceases to be an existence, to become a relation.
It ceases, also, to possess a positive moral valuation.
The State will be good when this relation is just,

bad when unjust. It is no longer a super-individual or trans-individual agent. It can no longer "will itself," or justify its will in the fact of being the good in itself. It has no will. Furthermore, it is not possible to speak seriously of a will that wills itself. The most selfish man in the world cannot will himself ; he wills the things that please him. Every act of will is transcendental ; it passes from a subject to an object which cannot be the same subject. But this kind of criticism is very recent in Germany. The German people is still actuated by the Hegelian conception which identifies the State with the good. Thoughts have frequently the queer property of not becoming motive feelings until they have faded away from one's consciousness. If you ask me to explain why such cultured men as Germans usually are let themselves be thrown like dumb stone against the Verdun trenches, without being stimulated by the conviction that they were fighting for a just cause, as in the war against Napoleon, I shall answer you in two words : Hegel's heresy.

But the greatest heresy of Hegel is only the amplification, to the point of absurdity, of Kant's initial heresy. To Kant the action of the State is heteronomous, in contrast to the autonomous or free action of the individual. The reason is that Kant believed in the existence of things in themselves, and therefore the identity he establishes between the conditions of the knowing subject and those of the known object is only a relative one ; for Kant believed not only in that which is known about things, but in the things themselves. Hence, in his ethics he distinguishes between the actions we carry out spontaneously and those which we carry out in obedience to social coercion or regulation. The latter are legal, and the former moral.

In Hegel's absolute idealism there are no things
in themselves. That is why his ethics begins in
legality and culminates in the State. In Hegel's
idea everything is autonomous. Things are nothing
but the position, or, rather, the negation, of the
idea when it comes out of itself. But this concept
of autonomy was not invented by Hegel, but by
Kant himself, when he said that ethics was not
based on the concept of the good, but on the
autonomy of the will—or, in other words, when
he identifies the liberty of the agent with goodness
and tells us that every free action is good because
it is free.

Both the ethics of Hegel and that of Kant are
formalist in so far as they determine the goodness
of an action, not by its content, good or evil, but
by its agent. If the agent, whether the individual
or the State, is autonomous, the action is good.
Now, ethic formalism, with its cult of autonomy
(self-government), has as a necessary consequence
the cult of force. So far as I know, this accusation
has never been brought against formal ethics.
Nevertheless, it is undeniable. Why? Because
autonomy is the faculty of acting with spontaneity,
and without giving way to impulses external to
the agent. This faculty presupposes force. Formal
ethics may be interpreted in an individualistic sense.
In this case it will lead us to wish not that the
individual shall serve the good, but that he shall be
the master ; that he shall possess strength. The
practical result of this ethics will be a society in
which each individual will take care only to increase
his own strength ; and, as this cannot be done
without diminishing that of the others, we shall
arrive, in this way, at the war of every one against
every one, as Hobbes described the natural State.
But, if we give to formal ethics the Hegelian inter-

pretation, our ideal will be a State, which, again, will not seek to serve the good, but only to be master, to assure its autonomy, and to increase its strength. And as the State has no existence or will, the practical result of this ideal will be a society, in which the will of the rulers—who will appropriate to themselves the name of the State— will reign despotically over that of the ruled, since the ruled will not merely be subject in the material sense to the ruling machinery, but will, above all, be subject to it morally ; for they will be convinced that the first social virtue is that of obedience to the State, which, in fact, means obedience to the rulers.

Now, a State based on the supreme autonomy of the rulers, which implies the absolute obedience of the ruled, would end by destroying itself if it were alone in the world, for the masses of it would be crushed and annihilated not so much by oppression, but by the very lack of hope of ever ameliorating their lot ; and once the masses were crushed the rulers would be left either without any ruled to rule, or with a mass of pariahs so utterly dispirited through the hopelessness of ever achieving freedom, that they would have left neither vitality nor the ambition necessary to carry on the ordinary work of industrial life. A man would not attend to a machine for eight hours a day for ten years, and retain the necessary interest in his work to do it well, if he had not the lingering hope of one day being out of it. Only by struggling with other States could such a State be saved, through the conquest and incorporation of other States ; for, as it extended its boundaries, its governing class would increase at the same time—and by that means the oppressed could always feed upon the hope of themselves one day becoming oppressors. Such is the secret of Prussia. Her vitality depends on her successive expansion in concentric circles of domination, which opens to the worst-treated Prussians the prospect of converting themselves into the tyrants of newly conquered countries. Formal ethics contributes in its turn to the realization of these ends and to increase the power of the State, in so far as it unites the ruled under the command of the rulers; and it is well known that union makes strength.

We have, then, face to face two possible interpretations of formal ethics: the authoritarian or " statist," and the liberal or individualistic. The first will produce societies which will think only of increasing the power of the State, that is to say, of the rulers; and the second societies which will think only of increasing the power of the individuals. In a conflict between both types of society victory will fall to the lot of the authoritarian and defeat to the individualistic, for the simple reason that the forces of the former will be united and those of the latter disunited. If it does not happen that the authoritarian societies are governed by fools, who try to dot the p's instead of the i's, there is no doubt that they must prevail over the individualistic societies; for in the latter, if individualism is absolute, there will be no union even for common defence; and even after such societies have seen their very existence threatened it is possible that there may be innumerable fools who, instead of hastening to defend them, will prefer to pride themselves on their pacifist convictions.

But an absolutely individualistic society has never existed, nor is it possible for one to exist. Formal ethics is false, for the goodness of man, be he ruler or ruled, does not consist in maintaining his autonomy but in realizing the good. Man is not an end; he is a means to the good.

God has given man a will, not as an end in itself, but to enable him to compel Nature, who has no will, to serve the good as far as possible. In this mission man finds the true basis of his associations. Placed between material and spiritual things, the isolated man is powerless either to manage the first or to realize the second. For this purpose men associate ; but they associate in material things to realize the spiritual. No new mystic kind of will rises with the association. The association has no will. An association which wills itself cannot exist. When it is said that such a thing exists, what really does exist is a combination of rulers of the association who seek to increase their power. There is no other will than that of the individuals. A common will does not exist. What exists is the common thing willed by a plurality of wills. And when this common thing is good, the association is good. From this goodness of the common thing is derived the discipline of every association. Because the common thing is good those associated ought to serve it. And when this common thing is defence against unjust violence and aggression, this common thing ought to hold absolute sway over the arbitrariness of individuals. The sole legitimate authority is not that of the Pope or that of the emperor or the individual, but that of the good. Other authorities are only legitimate when they serve the good ; and they cease to be so when they cease to serve it.

With this objectivization of morality, every kind of subjectivism, individual or trans-individual—and with it the whole of the German heresy—is overpowered. But it is an easy thing, and not urgent, to refute Germany in theory. What is important is to refute her in practice. And that can be done only by cannon shots.

A DOCTRINE OF POWER

SOME day there will have to be written a
" Cratology," or doctrine of human power, as
distinguished from " Energetics," or the doctrine
of power in general ; for if such a work is left
unwritten we shall find this question of power
encroaching upon problems of morals, or law, and
of politics, throwing both them and us into
confusion. The pure theories of morals, of law,
and of politics, can and must turn our eyes away
from power ; for they do not need it to tell us
what things are good, what other things are laws,
and what other good things it is desirable to secure
for ourselves by means of the law. But we cannot
theorize on morals, law, and politics without having
our thoughts fixed on the application of our theories
to the practical affairs of life ; and such application
is impossible without power.

Thus we find explained the double phenomenon
—why the " Cratology " has not yet been written,
and why writers on morals, law, and politics have
given up so many pages to the task of finding
out how it is possible to obtain the power to carry
theories of morals, law, and politics into practice.
This doctrine of power has not been dealt with
because the writers have seen, and with reason,
that power is only a means for the application
of moral or political ideas and of legal rules. A
" Cratology " cannot be, in theory, more than a
secondary doctrine, since it is a doctrine of the

means and not of the ends.   On the other hand, this explains the interest taken by so many writers in the problem of power ;   because they are here dealing with the possibility of their ideas being practically applied.   Power is the only means of making laws, good or bad, and of performing actions, good or bad, legal or illegal ;   but it is, on the other hand, the necessary and inevitable means—so necessary and inevitable that it leads many authors to assure that power is the very basis of law, of morals, and of politics.   Instead of investigating what law is, and what good things are, and what good things ought to be secured by law, these people seek to ascertain where the sovereign power lies, or to know who defines the things which are good, or where public power ought to be—whether in the many, or in the few or in a single person.

But if, so far as authors are concerned, power is nothing more than a means of realizing political or moral ideas, we find ourselves, in real life, confronted with the indisputable fact that a large number of human actions are not planned for the realization of political, juridical, or moral ends— that in them, in fact, energy is not merely the means but the end also.   Most people would prefer at times to accumulate energy, in the form of money, for example, or muscular strength, for the pleasure of accumulating it ;   and at other times to expend it in enjoyment for the pleasure of expending it. And that fact has led the Italian philosopher, Benedetto Croce, to suppose (in his " Philosophy of the Practical ") that there exists a special activity of the practical spirit—an activity which he calls " economic "—in which he includes the political and juridical activities, as distinguished from the " moral " activity.   The aim of the former is utility, energy, pleasure ; and of the latter, righteousness, goodness, duty. The reasons why, this autonomy of the " economic " activity ought not to be accepted are given by the same Croce when he says that " When the moral consciousness arises, utilitarian volitions lose the right to innocence," and that " morality claims absolute sway, over life." Moral consciousness is a fact. We no longer live in the Garden of Eden, but in a world which divides things into good and bad. Therefore we thrust aside Croce's " Economics " from this Kingdom of Ends, in which we accept his Logic, his Æsthetics, and his Ethics, for the matter of Croce's " Economics " is power, and power is an ethical, an æsthetical, and a logical instrument, and not an end, not a good in itself ; but we warmly recommend its study to every, man interested in the problem of power.

It may be said that the cause of Benedetto Croce's perplexity consists in the fact that he has set forth, but not solved, the problem of Cesare Borgia. Croce admires Borgia for his energy, but he detests him for the manner in which he applies it. And as Croce cannot get rid either of his admiration or of his horror, he ends by legitimizing both feelings, upholding the autonomy of the activity which he calls " economic " before the ethical activity. And it is true that this " economic " activity is a fact. It is a fact. Who does not know among his own acquaintances a score of little Borgias ? But the right to an " economic " activity, opposed or indifferent to the moral, cannot be admitted, for the simple reason that a fact is not a right. The whole meaning of culture consists precisely in finding a way, of taming the Borgias. Borgia's greatest admirer was Machiavelli ; but the meaning of Machiavelli's work must be sought in the last chapter of the " Prince ": " Exhortation to liberate Italy from the barbarians." It is only in this work of liberating Italy from the barbarians that Cesare Borgia can acquire any moral value. Until then he is only a considerable amount of natural energy let loose upon the world.

A " Cratology " would first divide human energy into personal power and social power. Personal power might also be called natural power, for we receive it from Nature and not from society. Society may give us money, position, means of education, and other advantages which may all be formulated in terms of power. But there are powers of activity, of talent, of will, and of health which we receive from Nature in varying quantities. Some men more than others. That is inevitable. We should all like to possess the maximum amount of personal power. That is also inevitable. We all envy the men who possess more personal power than we ourselves do. Inevitable, too. If a doctrine of personal power were written, the fools would study it with the same avidity as that with which they now read those newspaper advertisements that promise them energy or the gift of command or the cure of timidity. Wise men, on the other hand, would not see in this part of the " Cratology " anything more than a systematization of the numerous experiences which teach us not to waste our energy in excesses, to take care of our health, to concentrate our thoughts, etc.

How shall it be denied that personal power is required by the saint for his sanctity, by the artist for his art, and by the rascal for his rascality, and that power is an instrumental good? The feeling of possessing the power necessary for accomplishing our work is, too, one of the greatest pleasures, just as there are few feelings of anguish so painful

as that of knowing that we are not able to reach
our goal. And not only that. We should all like
to possess a quantity of free energy—that is to
say, energy independent of that needed for carrying
out the work we have in hand and works to follow ;
energy that we could waste at our own caprice, in
gambolling, in bursts of laughter, in the pure
pleasure of using it up. More: the possession of
free energy is much more agreeable to us than
that which we have mortgaged in the work we
have undertaken. As soon as we set about a piece
of work seriously, all our energy seems to us to
be too little to accomplish it ; and the fear that
we may not be able to do what we wish to do
is inevitably felt by every man who is doing something good. Hence the reason why play is more
beautiful than work.

But if free energy is the more pleasant, it is not
with it, but with the enchained energy, that all the
good things in the world have been made. It is
the same with the natural energy of man as with
the energy of Nature. Waterfalls served no human
purpose until mills were built and turbines invented
to transform energy into work. Perhaps the whole
tragedy of man lies in this fatal conflict between
the freedom and the enchainment of energy. We
like free energy better. But the making of a good
thing implies the binding of our energy to this
work. Free energy is not bad in itself. It is
neither good nor bad, but indifferent ; like matter,
like life. The point is that energy cannot be good
except when it is bound up in good works ; and
it cannot be so bound up when it has been wasted.
And as the idea that we have been born to do
something good in the world is always present,
more or less clear, in every mind, innocence in
regard to the employment of personal power is no

longer possible. Either we employ it in good works, in which case we receive from the work itself the recompense for having expended our power, or we waste it in vanities or bad works, and then no compensation is possible. Our confessor may absolve us, but his absolution does not bring back to us our wasted energy.

But the most interesting side of a " Cratology " would not be that of personal power, but that of social power—that is to say, the power that society puts into our hands, be it money or university degree or hereditary position or the command of a regiment or the leadership of a political party or anything else. Almost every man occupies a position of social power besides his personal power. And it is not difficult to distinguish between them. A sculptor, for example, cannot possess the marble necessary for his monument except when society has given it to him ; his personal power consists in that energy which he utilizes in carving his figures, or which he wastes on his own caprices, in accordance with the character of the man. And here arises the problem of whether it is better to grant social power to men with full liberty for them to employ it as they like, or whether it is better to make this concession of power conditional on the execution of a specific social function. The world still remembers with horror the Kaiser's speech at the swearing-in of the new recruits at Potsdam on November 23, 1891 :—

" Recruits: Before the altar and before the ministers of God you have sworn the oath of fealty to me. You are too young fully to understand the significance of what has been said. Your first duty is blindly to obey every order and every command. You have sworn fealty to me. You are the men of my Guard and my soldiers. You have committed

4

yourselves to me body and soul. There can be but one enemy for you, and that is whoever shall be my enemy. Owing to the present machinations of the Socialists it may happen that I shall order you to fire on your own relatives, on your brothers and on your fathers—God grant it may not be—and in that case you are bound to obey my orders blindly."

What is it that revolts us in this document? Is it only the fact that a man may exercise such enormous power over other men? No; it is not that. Any one who remembers the proclamations issued by General Joffre on the eve of the battles of the Marne and of Champagne will realize that the powers of the French generalissimo are not less, for certain determined ends, than those of the German Emperor. It could not be otherwise; for in war unity in the command is essential. What does revolt us in the Kaiser's speech and in the constitution of the German Empire is the fact that the powers of the Emperor are not bound down to a specified function or moment, while the powers of General Joffre are restricted to the operations of a war the cause of which his men believe to be a just one. No man can carry out a social work if society does not confer upon him the powers necessary for doing so. But it is one thing to give an explorer the resources he requires for reaching the Pole, and quite another thing to give him a cheque to spend as he may wish. In the first case we are creating an objective right, bound to a function; in the second, a subjective right, free and arbitrary. In the first case it is always possible to revoke the rights or powers conceded, as certainly those of General Joffre would be revoked if he employed them in sacrificing the lives of his soldiers uselessly. But subjective rights are, by definition, irrevocable. They can be withdrawn only by force —revolutions or *coups d'état*.

It is obvious that society ought never to grant powers to anybody, except when they are attached to a defined function. The fact that an efficient general is entitled to as many men and supplies as may be necessary for him to carry on a war to a successful conclusion is not a reason why, for the sake of victory, he should have the right to spend as he wishes a certain amount of money. The same man who is able to utilize the services of a hundred thousand soldiers for social ends may not be able to spend a hundred thousand pounds except on unnecessary clothing for his wife or in satisfying the whims of his useless and vicious sons. Nevertheless, it is an old habit of all countries to pay with quantities of free energy for the services of men who have enchained their energies to social ends.

It is not difficult to understand the reason why. Nothing pleases us more than the free possession of social energy. It pleases us even more than the possession of personal energy ; for the wastrel who uses up his personal energy in pleasures knows that, at bottom, he is paying for this with his life, while the lady who amuses herself in tearing up a dress every day is paying for her pleasure not with her own life, but with the lives of the sempstresses who have been working for her. And as we all like the free possession of social energy, we suppose that it will also please those men who have rendered outstanding services to us: and thus is produced the paradox that countries pay men for the services they have rendered by enabling them and their descendants to leave off serving us if it suits them to do so. Thus are hereditary aristocracies constituted. Faust earns the gratitude of the labourers of a Baltic village because he builds a dam that defends their lands against coast erosion. And the labourers reward Faust by granting to him and to his descendants in perpetuity the right to exact a tax from them. Because a man has done something good, rights are granted to him which may enable his descendants to be bad with impunity. The spirit of solidarity creates, by gratitude, subjective rights, and afterwards these are turned against the solidarity in which they were born, until a type of man is produced, like the Kaiser, the Pope, or the perfect Liberal, who believes himself to be responsible only to God and to his own conscience for the use he makes of the social rights which he enjoys—and in this way peoples enslave themselves to the same men, or to the descendants of the same men, who in former times served them well, until new liberators arise, whom the liberated peoples will afterwards transform into tyrants.

This vicious circle will not be broken as long as peoples do not prefer government by things to government by men ; or, what amounts to the same thing, to bind social energy to social functions. This phrase as to being governed by things may be interpreted by a reader in bad faith in the sense of our being governed by the chairs we are sitting on. But these " things " of which we are speaking are not chairs, but justice, and kindness, and truth, and beauty ; and, if abstractions be found unpleasing, then those concrete things which are just or kind or true or beautiful. Either we submit to them, or we shall have to submit to the tyrant. And what is the tyrant? We have seen already : power set free. The conceptions of freedom and tyranny lose their antagonism in the analysis ; and the outcome is that they only define the same thing. Freedom is our own tyranny ; tyranny is the freedom of others.

There will never be an end of either tyranny or freedom. There will always be free energy in man, for there will always be free energy in Nature ; and the " physis " of man is that of Nature. Free personal energy will always be more abundant in youth than in maturity. Romantic poets are the flatterers of youth. But there is no merit in youth. To the best men it is only the melancholy age of vacillation. To all those who have made the good things that exist upon the earth there once arrived an hour in which a thing took possession of them, and in which they began to live for it alone—not for the glory, not for the success, but for the thing. And when the thing is good it projects upon the individual who did it that special nimbus which constitutes the dignity of man.

THE IDENTITY OF ECONOMIC AND MILITARY POWERS

As the centuries of the Middle Ages were spent in discussing, both by word and by sword, the question of the primacy of the spiritual or the temporal power, so have the political thinkers of the last few decades devoted their attention to establishing the primacy of military or economic power.

The problem has been formulated by thinkers of every intellectual school, but it has particularly interested those who have set out to seek remedies for the social injustices arising from the abuse of power. This is, generally speaking, the manner in which the problem has been set forth: They start from the assumption that the greater proportion of men are exploited and oppressed by the remainder ; and they ask whether men are exploited because they are oppressed, or whether they are oppressed because they are exploited. Those who believe that the roots of the evil lie in oppression deduce from this that not only oppression, but the exploitation (of man by man as well) would disappear with the excesses of authority ; and they thus inspire the programmes of the Liberal parties of men, who call themselves Radicals, Syndicalists, or Anarchists. Those, again, who believe that the origin of injustice lies in exploitation come to the conclusion that not only injustice but also oppression, would disappear with the iniquities of capitalism ; and they urge the supporters of the Socialist parties to concentrate their attention, in the first place at least, on the economic problem.

Controversy becomes obscure when, instead of speaking of military power, which is a definite thing, it deals with political power, which is confused and composite. Political power is nowadays a mixture of spiritual power or the influence which the propagandist of an idea exercises on his followers ; of economic power, with the aid of which a body of plutocrats can make themselves masters of the machinery of one or more political parties ; and of the implicit military power possessed by, the leaders of large groups of men, since it is always possible for such leaders to make use of their followers, more or less, in defending their interests by means of physical force. As political power may always be resolved into its three component parts of spiritual power, material economic power, and material military power, the question of the primacy of one material power over the other may be simplified and reduced to its elements if we regard it as the primacy of economic or military power.

Most people, without troubling themselves over-much about the controversies of the intellectuals, endeavour to solve the problems of the abuse of power by their own common sense as these problems arise, without investigating their real origin. Thus the Socialist parties, taking their stand on the ideological supposition that the origin of human oppression lies in exploitation, and being confronted in the last few years with the problem of increasing military expenditure, have proposed as a solution, in France and Germany, the plan of a democratic citizen army, in which the officers would be elected by the soldiers, as the only means of safeguarding the liberty of the people in the face of aggression from abroad and militarism at home.

This plan is an excellent one ; at any rate, in its general lines. But there is not the slightest probability of carrying it into effect so long as the German military caste retains its power—that military caste which, " holding Germany, in its grip, had resolved to make war upon Europe," to use Mr. Hyndman's expression. For that reason a few sincere Socialists, such as Mr. Hyndman and Mr. Blatchford, who, without paying much attention to the economic interpretation of history, and without giving up their ideal of a citizen army, expressed their belief that the most urgent problem, if not the most important, of European democracy lies in making preparations to resist the aggression arising from the German menace.

It cannot be denied that in thus urging the people of England to prepare to resist German aggression these Socialist leaders showed that they had their eyes open, since they had become aware of the existence of realities which contradicted their doctrines, and that they had the necessary courage to defend opinions which could not but be unsympathetic to their followers and colleagues—men who had habituated themselves to forgetting the disagreeable fact that military power still survived in the world. Both of them thereby justified their position as political leaders and as practical men. But did they not at the same time contradict their position as thinkers ?

Mr. Hyndman is a thinker attached to his " theories," to his " economic analysis," and to his " historical investigations." Mr. Hyndman is the most eminent defender, in England, of the Marxian theory ; and he has recently devoted an article (in the *English Review*) to hailing " The Coming

Triumph of Marxist Socialism "—the very article in which he speaks of "the militarist caste which, holding Germany in its grip, had resolved to make war upon Europe." And this will not do. You cannot speak of the coming triumph of Marxism when at the same time you begin to recognize the fact that a military caste, resolved upon making war on Europe, holds Germany in its grip. This is like recognizing the vision of God on Sinai and writing immediately afterwards about the coming triumph of atheism ; or maintaining the infallibility of the Pope and then starting to criticize his encyclicals.

For the essential principle of Marxism is that economic power is held to be superior to politico-military power. No one now disputes the fact that Marx must be acknowledged as the real inventor, although self-contradictory, of the economic interpretation of history. From that theory, springs the originality of his "Misère de la Philosophie" and of his first really scientific book, "Zur Kritik der Politischen Œkonomie." It is the supposition upon which the four volumes of his "Kapital" are based. The possibility of a capitalistic society finding itself in the grip of a military caste never occurred to Marx at all. On the last page of his "Kapital" he tells us that the three great social classes are the wage-earners, the capitalists, and the landowners ; and nowhere does he speak of the military caste or class. In the Communist Manifesto we find the words: "The Executive of a modern State is but a Committee for managing the common affairs of the bourgeoisie."

In "Das Kapital" we may read: "In the direct relation of the possessor of the means of production to the direct producers—a relationship the forms of which always correspond naturally to a given stage in the methods and conditions of the work, and, consequently, to its social productivity—we may find the secret, the hidden bases, of the entire social structure and also of the political organization." And it was not that the Marxists passed unnoticed the opposed theory of the primacy of military power. They, indeed, had to force their way through the theory as it was maintained by Dühring. The whole of the central part of Frederick Engels' " Anti-Dühring," one of the classical books of Marxism, is devoted to a refutation of the Gewalts-theorie, the theory of force, according to which " the formation of political relations is the historic fundamental, and economic adjuncts are merely an effect, or a special case ; and always, therefore, secondary facts." The reader must note that, as the title of his theory suggests, political power for Dühring is military power. " The prime factor," said Dühring, " must always be sought in imme-diate political power and not in an indirect economic power." And he illustrated his thesis with an allegory in which the exploitation of man by man began on the day that Robinson Crusoe, dagger in hand, made a slave of Man Friday.

Of the economics of Robinson Crusoe we know only what a novel tells us, and there are varying opinions regarding what took place in primitive societies ; but in the case of modern Germany it would appear that Mr. Hyndman is right when he tells us that she is in the grip of a military caste. What has become of Herr Ballin? The motto of the Hamburg-Amerika Line said proudly, some time ago, " The world is my field " (" *Mein Feld ist die Welt* "). But its ships are now humbly wait-ing until the English Navy permits them to sail the seas again. What has become of the great German industrial and banking magnates? The

generals in the field ask the Berlin Government
for supplies and money ; and the Government asks
the bankers and industrialists. The German Government has put an end to the economy of exchange
—so far as wheat is concerned, and consequently
to so much capitalism—and has reverted to a régime
of natural economy wherein the people produce what
they consume. Far from the executive power being
a committee of the bourgeoisie, the entire German
bourgeoisie appears to be nothing but an adjunct
of the army commissariat.

It will be said that we are in a period of war.
But in times of peace the same thing happens.
When the military power of Germany demands men
and money, the bourgeoisie—even the Socialists—
hasten to give what is asked for, as they do now.
As Germany adds to her armament so do other
nations. And all the large States would seem to
have entered into an agreement to corroborate
Dühring's principle that natural economic laws can
show their effects only within the frame within which
they are confined by the military power.

In spite of this, Dühring was vanquished. While
the followers of Marx and Engels were increasing
like the flocks of the patriarchs, Dühring died a
solitary death, unknown, and a prey to the persecution mania. It was partly a fault of style.
Dühring's arrogant, pompous, and heavy manner
of writing could not compete with the Miltonic power
of Marx's prose. It was partly also a fault of the
times. Dühring's philosophy was idealistic when
the classic days of idealism were past and before
the days of its resurrection had begun to dawn.
The philosophy of Marx and Engels was materialistic, like their epoch. And the working classes
were tired of the political agitations and romantic
beards of 'forty-eight.

But what greatly helped to rout Dühring was the fact that Engels was able to answer him with excellent arguments—that, in the case of Crusoe, it was not only with the dagger that Friday was enslaved, but by Crusoe's possession of land and the other instruments of production and the means of sustenance ; that war and its instruments cost a great deal of money ; that " violence does not create money, but, at the utmost, only takes possession of wealth already created ; and even this does not bring much advantage with it, as we have found out, to our sorrow, as the result of the French millions "., ; and that nothing depends so much upon economic pre-conditions as do the army and navy, whose equipment, composition, organization, tactics, and strategy are regulated, above all, by the means of production and communication to such an extent that the Prussian General Staff laid down the principle : " The basis of a military organization must primarily be sought in the economic constitution of the people."

And this war of artillery, aeroplanes, submarines, railways, trenches, and economic pressure will not give the lie to this principle. What enables the belligerents to maintain in the line of fire such enormous masses of fighting men, who consume such great quantities of supplies, is the fact that they have at their command large amounts of capital accumulated in preceding generations.

This is apparently a contradictory conclusion. Military matters move within the economic frame —and Marxism is right. Economics moves within the limits laid down by the military power—and Dühring is right. Economics is the essential, military power is the essential. But why cannot both be essential ? Why cannot Dühring be as right as Marx ? We cannot think of the totality of powers otherwise than as a traffic of substances which condition one another. The definition of a power includes its effects on other powers. When, therefore, Marx, a man of a more practical spirit than Dühring, sets himself to investigate the dynamics of oppression, it is natural that he should trace its roots to exploitation. It is equally explicable why Dühring, who was more of a theorist than Marx, sought the origin of exploitation and found it in violence. In the reciprocal action and reaction of different powers it is logical enough that each of them should appear to us to be conditioned by the others. But there is no logical necessity for affirming the primacy either of the economic power or of the military power.

There is, on the contrary, a simple reason why one should not speak of the primacy of military or economic or political power. It is that arms, wealth, and political position are only different manifestations of power. Power is one, its forms are many. The same thing happens with natural energy : although it is one, it appears to us in different forms as gravitation, electricity, magnetism, colour, light, or chemical affinities. And the proof that social power is one and the same thing is seen in the fact that its different manifestations may be transformed into one another. The history of modern Prussia is that of the transformation of a military into an economic power. In present-day England the economic power has been transformed into a military one. The antithesis established by Herbert Spencer between an industrial and a warlike State is superficial. Where there is industry there is a possible army ; where there is an army there is potential industry. In both cases there is power. But it is not enough that power should exist : the important thing is for it to be distributed according to the principles of justice, and for it to constitute the machinery of which society may avail itself for the production of cultural values.   Hence the necessity of clearly studying the relation between the concepts of power, right, and culture.

RIGHT AND MIGHT

I

THE PACIFIST THEORY.

IT may be affirmed unreservedly that men do not stand in need of any philosophy to distinguish might from right. They know quite well that there are acts of might which are at the same time of right, such as the Civil War in the United States, waged by the North to secure the emancipation of the slaves ; and that there are acts of right which are at the same time of might, such as the Edict of Milan, by which Constantine granted to the Christians civil rights and toleration throughout the Empire. But they also know that there are acts of might which are not of right, such as the violation of Belgian neutrality by the Germans ; and that there are ideas of right, such as those defended by the Liberals of Germany and the English Chartists in 1848, which do not attain actuality because they are not maintained by sufficient might. Might is a condition of all historical realities. Right is, on the other hand, only the property of some realities. Some realities of might are according to right ; others against right, and others indifferent. These are the words of common sense.

This is simply saying that the relation between might and right is contingent or historical, to use

Rickett's terminology ; or external, if we prefer the language of Messrs. Moore and Bertrand Russell, and of the Americans, Holt, Marvin, Montague, Perry, Pitkin, and Spaulding. It is an external relation because the concept of right does not contain that of might, or the concept of might that of right. When we say that bodies are subjected to the action of gravitation, it may possibly be said that this is an internal relation, because the idea of body is, perhaps, contained in that of gravitation, and the idea of gravitation in that of body. But although might and right are united in specified acts, this union is brought about only in historical or accidental individual wholes, and only in the idea of God this union becomes unity. Logically, might and right form two distinct and incongruous elements, two universals, two " ultimates."

But the English theory of external relations, and Rickett's theory of historical individuals, although old as the world and clear as common sense, are too new in modern science to begin to operate as revolutionary leaven in the world of politics, ethics, law, economics, and education. The theory which still pervails in moral sciences, in Germany especially, tends to unify might and right, either by saying that right is might, or by asserting that might is right. The first is the theory that we shall call pacifist ; the second, militarist.

The pacifist theory *must* consist of two postulates : the first, that right is in itself might ; and the second, derived from the former and included in it, that might has no real existence independently of right. I say that it *must* consist. What I mean is that it *should* consist if the pacifists could think logically. It is an obvious fact that most pacifists acknowledge the existence of right as distinct from might ; and that their theory only asserts that right *ought* to overcome might. But in making these assertions, with which I agree, they cease to be pacifists ; for, if might is something other than right, they can no longer believe that right has any influence on might, for a point of contact is lacking to these two elements ; and more than half a century ago—if the metaphor may be forgiven—Faraday denied the possibility of action at a distance. To assert that might is a different thing from right, as the pacifists generally do, is equivalent to asserting that right cannot influence might, and that unjust might can be opposed only by just. But when he makes this last assertion the pacifist has ceased to be such.

Let us imagine the case of a radical pacifist, in a country of obligatory military service, who is ordered by the authorities to join a regiment. The pacifist believes that this order is an act of unjust force. He may do one of three things : obey the order of the authorities, resist passively, or resist actively. If he obeys, he proves by his own act the powerlessness of unarmed right in the face of might ; if he resists passively he proves it also, since he is only taken to a prison instead of to a regiment ; and if he resist actively he acknowledges that might employed in the service of injustice can be combated only by forces employed in the service of justice. He will have proved in the three cases that might and right have no point of contact.

To which the pacifist may answer that they have, indeed, a point of contact, and that this point is the consciousness of man. But in saying this they only carry the question to another stage. If consciousness is something simple it cannot comprise two elements like might and right, which are heterogeneous, according to our supposition ; or if consciousness is something composite, there is not the slightest reason to suppose that two heterogeneous elements such as right and might can act in consciousness one on the other. It is all the same whether might and right are placed in the sphere of objective things or in the sphere of consciousness. If they are two things of separate quality they cannot act one on the other. The pacifist who thinks of them as distinct thereby acknowledges that right cannot act on might, and he ceases therefore to be a pacifist, since he finds himself in contradiction with himself.

I realize that if these lines reach the hands of the Hon. Bertrand Russell he will be surprised to find his logical doctrine of external relations turned against his cherished pacifist ideal. But this surprise is not at all surprising. There are many learned men who reason with accuracy on their own specialities, but who think with the utmost looseness on current topics ; who can reflect independently on abstruse subjects, but take their ideas on everyday matters ready-made from fourth-rate journalists. The present war has shown daily confirmation of this assertion ; and this strengthens our inclination to prefer the works to the men who make them.

We have come to the conclusion that the pacifist who analyses his concepts cannot believe that might and right are fundamentally different things without ceasing to be a pacifist. This obliges him, if he will not give up his pacifism, to seek a theory which shows that right is, in itself, might, and to deny that might is a reality insoluble in some other. Hence arise all these confused doctrines which deny the reality of evil, which say that brute force is only an appearance, a knocking at the door of the senses to awaken within us the consciousness of right, that at bottom there is no more reality than that of right, that might is only a shadow projected by right itself, and that non-resistance to evil is enough to assure in the long run the triumph of right.

If this vague and elegant verbiage were true, the pacifist idea would be absolutely unnecessary ; for war is only an appearance, violence is illusory ; there is no other reality than that of the good and of the right. The German shells in Belgium and in Serbia were only the raps given to itself by the consciousness of right ; eternal, unchangeable, like the peace of the absolute.

These things and others like them have been frequently said in England during the last few years. But the tragedy and the comedy of history led to this, that when England had to get ready to fight for her national existence the minds of many of her sons, especially in the democratic parties, were on the point of being submerged by a series of doctrines which closed their eyes to the vision of the great danger that threatened them. What is certain is that this pacifist doctrine is not of English origin, and much less of Liberal English origin. The English Liberals who carried out the Revolution in the seventeenth century did not believe that right prevailed by its own might in the world of historical realities. The English Puritan was militant. The Puritan, said Macaulay, " prostrated himself in the dust before his Maker ; but he set his foot on the neck of his king." And no one has found nobler accents in which to sing the employment of might in the service of right than the poet of " Samson Agonistes " :—

> O, how comely it is, and how reviving
> To the spirits of just men long oppressed,
> When God into the hands of their deliverer
> Puts invincible might,
> To quell the mighty of the earth, the oppressor,
> The brute and boisterous force of violent men. . . .

This historical or external junction of might and right was what enabled the English people to conqeur, preserve, or re-conquer their participation in the government at a moment when all the other European nations gave themselves up to the administration of absolute monarchies. The theory which subsumes might in right is certainly not English. It is German. It is Kant. It was formulated when Kant said, in his " Critique of Practical Reason," that the moral law must work (*muss wirken*) on the soul " (*im Gemüte*). This moral law is, in the Kantian philosophy, the very *noumenon* of freedom ; but not of the freedom of indifference, according to which we can do no good or evil, but of freedom understood as a kind of social regime in which we are not oppressed.

Kantian freedom is not free will, but the ideal of a liberal constitution : the Kingdom of the Ends. The Categorical Imperative makes us work in such a way that we use " Humanity, both in our own person and in the persons of others, not merely as a means, but at the same time as an end." And this Kingdom of the Ends is not merely an aspiration, but an actual reality which determines our actions. On this point the interpretation of Cohen is faithful to the Kantian doctrine : " In the same way as the being of the senses apparently chooses his actions, the good as well as the bad, when he finds himself, in truth, determined in this world, so the Thing-in-Itself, encamped behind the clouds of the empiric world, produces, with spontaneous originality, the phenomena which appear in the wings of the stage. . . ."

The characteristic of this ethic is the assertion that the moral law or Categorical Imperative must work, and does work, on the soul. But the fact is that it does not so work except occasionally. It is precisely the obviousness of evil and of brute force which has led some men to give their attention to moral problems. Why does the moral law work at some times? Why does it not work always? To these two antagonistic questions the Kantians have always given one and the same answer. The moral law works because it is "encamped behind the clouds of the empiric world." It works because it is *there*; it does not work always because it is enveloped in clouds.

This reply is logically indefensible. If the Imperative is categorical it must work always; if it does not work always it is not categorical. But the important thing is not the logical contradiction of this doctrine, but its practical results. For the Kantians say that when the moral law does not work it is because it is behind the clouds. And in consequence they have devoted their efforts to discovering it, for it was enough to discover it to make it work. In consequence, moral life has ceased to be practical and has been turned into pure speculation. And Kantianism has ended by substituting for "ethical culture" the "culture of ethics." Instead of asserting, as common sense does, that fighting for the right and the discovery of right are two different things, Kantianism has changed the fight into a discovery, and in that way it has eliminated the element of might.

This idealistic philosophy was spread through Germany in the first half of the nineteenth century. If it had been propagated among the princes, the Junkers, and the officers, its effects might perhaps have been beneficial, for we might possibly have witnessed the miracle of the tiger converted into a lamb. But it was propagated chiefly among the intellectual classes, who should have fulfilled the revolutionary function in Germany, and it gave an

essentially speculative character to their energies.
Hence arose all that enormous literature of idealistic
mysticism which is comparable, in quantity and
quality, only with that of the Alexandrians of the
third and fourth centuries. The intellectual value
of this literature is small. To it may be applied
the words of the Hon. Bertrand Russell :—

" What it calls knowledge is not a union with the
Not-Self, but a set of prejudices, habits, and desires,
making an impenetrable veil between us and the
world beyond. The man who finds pleasure in such
a theory of knowledge is like the man who never
leaves the domestic circle for fear his word might
not be law."

The practical result of this philosophy was the
collapse, perhaps final, of German Liberalism in
1848. The German Liberals forgot to convince
themselves that there was no other guarantee for
the realization of right in this word than its maintenance by force of arms. Only at the last moment
did it occur to the National Assembly of Germany
to nominate the Archduke Johann to the supreme
command of the Army. But it had not reckoned
either with the princes or with the troops. The
King of Prussia could say to the members of the
Assembly, " Do not forget that there are princes
in Germany, and that I belong to them." Prince, in
German, is not a vague word. " Fürst " means
first ; the first in power. A few months afterwards
four non-commissioned officers could dissolve the
National Assembly. And the result of that collapse
was expressed in the success of the Communist
Manifesto of Marx and Engels. The German people
ceased to believe in the heresy that right is in itself
might, and went over to the contrary conviction,
not less heretical and fatal, that might is, in itself,
right. The materialistic interpretation of history !

As the illusion that right could win by itself proved
to be deceptive, Germany passed to the belief that
everything that wins is right.

Radical pacifism, in asserting that right is in itself
might, is, in theory, a sin against truth, for it puts
" a set of prejudices, habits, and desires " in the
place of truth. But in practice it is a crime, for
it disarms right, and leaves it defenceless against
brutal aggression. But there are sins and sins,
crimes and crimes ; and the doctrine and practice
of pure militarism are a still graver sin and crime.

II

THE MILITARIST THEORY.

WE call the militarist theory that which says that
might is in itself right, and, therefore, subsumes the
concept of right in that of might. This theory is
upheld in Germany, first, by the most popular of its
ideologies, the " Monist," and, secondly, by the
most scholarly of its schools of Law, that represented
by Professor Jellinek, of the University of Heidelberg. I leave aside the influence which may have
been exercised on the formation of the German
mentality by independent writers such as Nietzsche
and Schopenhauer, or by semi-independent publicists
like Bernhardi. Neither Ostwald, the Pontifex Maxi-
mus of German Monism, nor Jellinek has ever said
that might is in itself right : how, then, can this
assertion be attributed to them? Simply by the
weight of logic. Our thesis will be sufficiently
proved if we can show that from certain principles
maintained by these men the inclusion of the
concept of right in that of might is practically
derived.

The most popular ideology of the New Germany is to be found in the Monist Sermons (*Monisten Predigten*) of Professor Ostwald. The secret of his success lies in his clearness. Ostwald confines himself to telling his readers that the times of religion have passed away, that men must now be guided by science, that there is nothing but energy in the universe, that every concept which does not refer to energy lacks content, and that human morality must be energetic, too. The great thought of Professor Ostwald consists in substituting for the Categorical Imperative of Kant his own Energetical Imperative, which says, "Do not waste energy, but give it a value."

These ideas are so simple of understanding that they are known in Germany as "Die Weltanschauung der Halbgebildeten," or, as one might say in English, the religion of the half-baked, if the concept of religion included also that of those people who believed in a God unconnected with goodness, like the Energy of Professor Ostwald. The historical reasons which have turned the German mind into a favourable field for the propagation of this "ethics" of the Energetical Imperative are well known: first, the religious wars of the sixteenth and seventeenth centuries in Germany were so bloody that they sowed in every mind the seeds of invincible repugnance towards all kinds of religious speculation; secondly, the fact that in the eighteenth century, when the New Germany was beginning to be formed, there was a prevalence of rationalistic materialism; thirdly, the difficulty or impossibility which the masses of the people found in understanding the philosophic terminology in which the idealistic reaction of Kant and Hegel against the materialism of the eighteenth century was expressed; and, fourthly, the need experienced by the people of filling the vacuum left in their souls by the economic interpretation of history. Marx and his followers gave to the Germans a theory of life. What they did not give them was an ethics. But ethics is necessary for action. We cannot take a single step forward without being guided by some criterion of right and wrong. Thus, in the absence of any other, the ethics of the Energetical Imperative was spread. Those who cannot understand how it was possible for such an extraordinary morality as that revealed by the present war to spring up in the centre of Europe should take the trouble of meditating for a few hours on the significance of the " Monist Sermons," which, some years ago, were being read in the barbers' shops and in the public-houses of Prussian towns.

For the postulate " All is energy ' amounts to the assertion that there is no right but might. It is true that Ostwald, side by side with the " bellum omnium contra omnes," which characterizes men in their natural state, recognizes also the existence of a natural law of sympathy and a feeling of solidarity. Ostwald says, in fact, that sympathy is a natural law, that is to say, something which must inevitably be realized. " The will of the Law cannot be other than one's own will," he says, in words that recall those of Kant. But this assertion is purely theoretical, in the sense that it applies only to the nature of our will, and does not provide us with a standard of conduct. That this assertion is false is proved by the present war : there would have been no war if human solidarity were a natural and inevitable law. But what Ostwald's Imperative commands is not that we shall serve human solidarity, but : " Do not waste energy ; give it a value."

If we had to analyse this Imperative we should

say one of two things : either energy cannot be
wasted, by virtue of the natural law of the conservation of energy ; or, if it can be wasted and valued,
one must admit the existence of evaluating ideas
—the old ideas of right and wrong ! which cannot
be reduced to energy, because they are qualities
and not quantities. Either the Energetic Imperative
is lacking in moral meaning and is a purely
utilitarian piece of advice, equivalent to saying :
" Don't spend your nights without sleeping " ; or,
if it has a moral meaning, it simply tells us : " Don't
use your energy for evil but for good "—with which
formulation I am in agreement, but which presupposes the existence of the ideas of right and
wrong, absolutely distinct from that of energy. In
this case it would recognize that the element of
morality works in the world as well as the element
of energy. But then the Monism of Prof. Ostwald
would no longer be a Monism but a dualism.

Let us now imagine the type of man who accepts
without criticism the Energetical Imperative. What
will he do if his only criterion is energy ? Either
he will devote himself exclusively to increasing his
own power—in which case he will become the
perfect egoist—or he will passively surrender his
own energy to a greater mass of energy, as a
river surrenders its waters to the sea—in which
case, of his own free will, he will accept his position
as one more workman of Krupp's, or as one more
soldier in the Kaiser's armies, as if it were his
natural fate.

But Ostwald's ideas cannot be considered as
representative of the German mentality precisely
because of their popular character. It is not so with
Professor Jellinek, of Heidelberg. Georg Jellinek,
until his death in 1911, was the highest authority in
German juridical thought. His theory of the State

is still the " official " theory. It is the organic theory which conceives the public power as the right of the State, and affirms the moral personality of the State. The reader need not be frightened by these words. German professors do not share my opinion that these questions of politics, law, and ethics are not technical questions, although they may be difficult, and ought not to be treated with a special terminology. German professors believe them to be technical questions, and they treat them with a vocabulary through which we have to find our way if we seek to refute the juridical theory which they would like to impose on humanity—unfortunately not only with books.

I choose Jellinek because he is not at first sight a theorist of might. His conception of Law is that of the " ethical minimum which society needs at every moment of its life to go on living." From this conception of Law as the ethical minimum arises that of the State which realizes it. " The existence of Law depends on the existence of an organization which realizes it." Up to this point there is no objection to be made ; for State and organization—dangerous words—may be understood in the sense of government and administration—exact words. What is important for us is that Jellinek clearly distinguishes between the nature and the ends of the State. The nature of the State is might ; its end is morality. When this distinction is made, it would seem as if we were far removed from every theory which tries to consolidate might by urging the human mind to render obedience to it.

The nature of the State is defined by Jellinek thus : " The State is the unity of association, originally endowed with power of domination, and formed by men settled in a territory." In simpler language : the State is might. But in defining the ends of the State Jellinek says : " The State is the association of a nation, possessing a sovereign juridical personality which, in a systematic and centralizing way, availing itself of external means, promotes the individual, national, and human solidary interests in the direction of a progressive and common evolution." This means that the Government ought to be good, that might ought to serve right.

To distinguish between might and right is already to profess an ideal. That is why Jellinek stands out in Germany among the idealistic jurists. Some young men look in his books for principles which will enable them to put new life into Liberalism. But Jellinek is also the first of the upholders of the organic theory of the State, and this is the German theory—" the German idea." But the organic theory may adopt a crude form, as when Gierke says that " The State is a human-social organism with a life distinct from that of its different members." This theory is not accepted by Jellinek, because the State lacks the fundamental character of all living beings : renewal by the change of generations. Many modern States owe their existence to the sword ; and this is certainly not an organic means of procreation. Nor does Jellinek believe in the mystical character given by Hegel to his organic conception of the State when he defines it as : " A self-conscious moral substance, the rational and divine will which has organized for itself a personality." This belief in an ultra-material substance is rejected by Jellinek as metaphysical. To Jellinek the State : " Is the internal unity of a nation guided by one will."

But if the unity of the State is of an associative character, it is no longer of an organic character ; and it can no longer be said that Jellinek upholds the organic theory of the State. And yet he does uphold it. He upholds it when he says :—

"Every association needs a will which unifies it, and which cannot be other than that of the human individual. An individual whose will has the character of the will of an association ought to be considered, so long as this relation with the association subsists, as the instrument of its will, that is to say, as the organ of the association."

From this principle is derived the whole of Jellinek's organic theory. The organs of the State are divided into immediate and mediate. The immediate organ is what, in England, is called the Sovereign ; it may be a single individual, like the Kaiser, or a corporation, like the British Parliament. The mediate organs are formed by the different branches of the bureaucracy. The immediate organ is completely independent ; that is to say, it is not subject to the will of any other. The plurality of the immediate organs "is always menacing to the unity of the State and cannot last for long." "The State needs a unique will." "Every State needs a supreme organ." "The organ, as such, has no personality in face of that of the State." "There are not two personalities, that of the State and that of the organ ; but State and organ are rather a unity." While in the representative theory, "representatives and represented are always two, the association and the organ remain at every moment the same person." "The organs never become persons : chiefs of State, Chambers, authorities, have never a juridical personality ; the sole and exclusive personality belongs to the State." "The organ has no rights, and only juridical competence." Thus "disappears the doctrine of the right of the monarch to the power of the State." "This power belongs to the State, and the monarch, as such, is the supreme organ of the State." " On the other hand, the individual may have the right to occupy the place of an organ." " If the organs of the State were eliminated, there would only remain, juridically speaking, nothing-ness."

Such is " the German idea." Every State requires a unique will. A unique will requires a supreme organ. If this supreme organ and this unique will be suppressed, juridically only nothingness remains. This is the " official " doctrine of Germany. In Russia there is the fact of the absolutism of the Tsar. But the intellectual classes protest. It is in Germany that political science and the universities proclaim the supreme organ and the unique will.

This theory is based on the assertion that : " Every association needs a will which unifies it, and which cannot be other than that of the human individual." In these lines is condensed the whole system of German obedience and docility. But the assertion which they express is false. It is not true to say that every association needs a will which unifies it. The characteristic feature of every association is the plurality of wills. There are as many wills as individuals in the association. If it were true that without a unifying will there could be no associations, we should have to deny the existence of associations, for that of the plurality of wills cannot be denied.

Nevertheless, every association presupposes unity. Where lies the source of the unity of associations? We have seen that it is not in the will, for the very simple reason that wills cannot become united in one without disappearing. But it is not necessary for wills to be united in one in order that they may associate themselves. That in which wills associate themselves is a common object. This common object may be to play football or the desire of self-government. But it is the common thing and not the unique will which is the basis of associations.

By basing the association on a unique will, Jellinek has to found his State upon an "originary power of domination." That is basing right on might. It is not enough to say subsequently that this might ought to be employed in the service of right. That is entrusted to the conscience of the individual who is acting as the "supreme organ" of the association, or to the mediate organs. The members of the association have no other function than that of acknowledging the necessity of the "unique will" and the "supreme organ," and obeying them.

But this theory is false. The true essence of associations does not lie in the unique will, but in the common thing. Things unite men. And that is why, in face of domineering wills, Democracy is still possible.

THE ECONOMIC INTERPRETATION OF HISTORY

WE have mainly spoken of the ideas that have made possible the constitution of the German State and, consequently, the actual war. We are now going to deal with the material factors or class interests that have found in these ideas a justification of every kind of action by means of which they could achieve their ends. But in doing so we must avoid the danger of falling into one of the most popular and pernicious expressions of modern romanticism and subjectivism: the so-called " economic interpretation of History." I say, popular, because I very much doubt whether such a thing seriously exists in the world of science. It is true that from some passages in Marx it may be logically deduced, and it has been deduced, that he believed that the chief cause of social changes is the economic factor. These phrases are well known: " In the immediate relations of the master of the conditions of production with the immediate producers . . . we find the inmost secret, the hidden bases, of the whole social fabric and of political institutions." " The manner of production of material life conditions, in general, the process of social, political, and spiritual life." " The hand-mill gives you society with the feudal lord ; the steam-mill society with the industrial capitalist."

These and similar phrases convince us that Marx really believed in the " economic interpretation of

History." What has not been sufficiently said is that Marx likewise believed in another and completely opposed theory, which may be formulated as " the historical interpretation of Economics." Marx has repeatedly maintained that " every, economic institution is an historical category." His criticism of " classical " Economics is based precisely on the fact that the economists have considered as " eternal " or natural categories what were purely " historical " or temporal categories. And these are not sentences taken at random. The desire to interpret Economics historically is as deep rooted in Marx as that of interpreting History, economically. His best work, " Das Kapital," is, at bottom, an historical investigation. I say at bottom because it may appear to be in form, as Marx acknowledges, an "a priori construction." But Marx denies that it is so, advising us to distinguish between his manner of exposition and his manner of investigation. In respect of his exposition he tells us that he has flirted (*kokettirte*) with the Hegelian dialectics. But the object of his " investigation was to appropriate the material in detail, to analyse its diverse forms of development, and to discover the inner bond uniting them." To do this is to write History. And when he comes to formulate the " secret " of capital or " original accumulation," he does it historically: " Expropriation of the English peasants. . . . Robbery of the goods of the Church. . . . Robbery of the State domains." Capitalism is, in the Marxist conception, an historical product, a creation of man, as accidental as the frontiers of Serbia or the parliamentary system. If afterwards he converts this into an entelechy, which moves according to its own laws and independently of human will, that is because Marx maintains the historical interpretation of

6

Economics, according to which Economics are determined by law, and law by the ideas prevailing in a given society, without giving up the economic interpretation of History, according to which law and ideas are results of economic conditions.

But the two interpretations mutually exclude one another. It is possible to conceive Economics and History in a process of mutual action and reaction, as members of a higher system. In this way we may conceive the relation which unites the planets Saturn and Neptune in our solar system. This is a relationship of reciprocity and not of causality. But in this relationship we cannot speak either of a Saturnian interpretation of Neptune or of a Neptunian interpretation of Saturn any more than we could speak of the economic interpretation of History or of the historical interpretation of Economics. This "interpretation" is possible only in a relation of causality. But in this case either Economics is the cause of History or History is the cause of Economics. Either one of these two propositions cancels the other.

You may ask me how it was possible for so great a thinker as Marx to fall into so clear a contradiction. I am not called upon to explain the contradictions of Marx. If I were, perhaps I should explain them by the fact that he was much more of an agitator and an historian than a thinker; perhaps to the fact that Marx, like a good Jew, possessed greater power of will than freedom of intelligence. But I repeat that I am not called upon to explain Marx's contradictions. Those who ought to explain them (and explain them away) are his followers. But they do not explain them; they accept them without being aware of them. It is said that the best defence of the economic interpretation of History is that of Mr. Edwin R. A.

Seligman, Professor of Economics at Columbia University. But at the end of his work I find this sentence: "The economic interpretation of History, by accentuating the historical bases of economic institutions, has done a great deal for Economics." Here we find accepted at the same time both the economic interpretation of History and the historical interpretation of Economics, without Mr. Seligman's suspecting the contradiction into which he has fallen.

There is, then, good reason to doubt whether a serious economic interpretation of History exists in the world of science. If it did exist, it would mean an attempt to interpret the objects of an individualizing science, such as History, through the objects of a generalizing science, such as Economics, as a rule, tries to be. History deals with individuals. These individuals may be as big or as little as you please. You may write a history of Julius Cæsar or of humanity, of Christianity, or of steam-engines; but it is inevitable that every history shall refer to an individual in the sense of something that is not divided. To interpret history economically is to look for the cause of the historic individual in economic generalities.

This attempt is, a priori, absurd. All things, organic or inorganic, have a general aspect common to other things of the same kind and an individual aspect particular and unique. The general aspect of a thing must be dealt with generically; the individual, individually. Generalizing sciences treat of the general; individualizing of the individual. History is the science of the individual. Why is it absurd to try to explain the individual through the general? Because the general is a condition, but not the cause of the individual. Every attempt to establish historical laws rests on a confusion

between the concept of condition and the concept
of cause. This confusion is very frequent in books
of science. But the reader will get rid of it if
he conceives the condition as a necessary but
insufficient causality to explain the individual, and
the true causality as that other which gives a
sufficient but not necessary explanation of the individual. The individual side of things is always
accidental. This word does not convey any
reproach. All things that we deem precious, every
cultural product, and the whole of culture itself
are accidental. It is within the bounds of possibility that culture may not survive the present war.

No general condition can explain the individual.
The fact that Julius Cæsar had to eat to live will
never explain Julius Cæsar. The history of Julius
Cæsar, like that of the Renaissance, like all history
—and I include that of an inorganic thing, such
as the moon—is that of an individual in so far as
he is not like other individuals. Hence the absurdity
of attempting to explain the historic individual
through a generalizing science such as Economics
pretends to be.

The absurdity disappears when Economics is converted into an historical discipline, content to explain
certain historical facts, such as markets, wages, rent,
capital, the growth in power of certain social classes,
overlooked by the usual historians. In this sense
the a priori construction of Economics may be conceived as a mere attempt to form empirical concepts
or nominal signs with which to apprehend certain
historical facts or certain aspects of historic material.
Thus conceived, general or theoretical Economics
is an ancillary science of history, such as Archæology
or Paleontology, while concrete Economics is converted into one of the modalities of History itself,
or into one of its parts, and certainly into one of

its most interesting parts, considering the important place occupied by Economics in human activities. But this is equivalent to saying that Economics or the History of the economical cannot interpret History in general, because the part cannot explain the whole ; and it would also be tautological to try to interpret History by History.

There are grave reasons for doubting that Economics can ever become a general autonomous science, and serve, as such, as a condition for History. A generalizing science becomes autonomous when it can formulate a natural or general law of its own. The only law which Economics can offer us with any claims to universality is that which defines the economic motive by saying that " every human being seeks to satisfy his needs with the minimum expenditure of effort." Even granting that this law were absolutely valid, it would not be economic but biological. We should not need Economics to formulate it, but should take it from Biology. We may safely say of a hungry tiger that if he sees a sheep three yards off he will not run ten miles to look for another. Of men, we can only say that this law is valid only in so far as it refers to their animal nature. In so far as they are men, we may say that they are the only animals which can drink when they are not thirsty, or leave off drinking when they are thirsty, or produce articles to satisfy desires that are not real needs, or waste the things they possess, or do not produce the things they really need.

The ultimate reason why natural economic laws do not exist—not even those which man could derive from his status as an animal ; that is to say, from biology—is that in biology the animal that tries to satisfy its needs with the minimum of effort i-

given by Nature itself, while in economics the factor
man is variable, because it is, in a certain measure,
voluntary. A German, Friedrich Naumann, who has
recently been much talked of in connection with
his book on Central Europe, has tried to make
population the basis of his economics in his book,
" New German Political Economy." According to
Naumann, the *primum movens*, the chief cause of
modern economic life, is the increase of population. That was written in April 1911. Two years
later, when he studied the figures of the German
birth-rate, he had to confess in his weekly paper,
Die Hilfe, that they revealed the fact that the mass
of the German nation was beginning deliberately
to refuse to perpetuate itself. This variability in
the factor man is what cancels also the " agrarian "
economics of Henry George, who attributes all evils
to the steady increase in land values. This increase
is an historical or accidental phenomenon, and not
a general law. The selling value of land in France
in 1879 was 89,000,000,000 francs, in 1913 it did
not exceed 68,000,000,000 francs. The cause of
this decrease must be sought in the lessening of
the birth-rate. But no doubt it was accompanied
by other and very complex causes.

Precisely because man is the most accidental or
the most historical of animals it is possible for
him, if not to annul the biological law, to evade
its fulfilment. On the one hand it is possible for
him to expend a much greater effort than that really
needed to satisfy his wants, because he has found
a source of pleasure in the effort itself through
love of the work. On the other hand, he has
discovered that if he can accumulate and stock more
articles than those he needs immediately, he frees
himself, in the sense that he enables himself to
devote his activities to non-material ends. Hence

arises a new interpretation of the economical. It is no longer a natural law but a value ; a product of culture. It is not an absolute value like that of the good or the true ; it is a conditional value, but always sufficient to enable us to understand the enthusiasm with which an Adam Smith contemplates the increase of wealth. Wealth frees man from the tyranny of immediate needs and allows him to be better. Neither hospitals, nor churches, nor museums, nor theatres, nor libraries could be built without wealth. And, nevertheless, we cannot interpret their construction economically. The economical does not enter into culture as an end, but as a means.

But the accidentality of men is so great that the economical, too, may rise to the category of an end. We all know the type of man to whom *les affaires sont les affaires*, and for whom business is the supreme measure of things. At times whole nations become contaminated by this ideal ; and even, strange hallucination ! console themselves for the poverty of their masses by exaggerating the millions of their rich men. Thus has arisen one of the most disconcerting illnesses of the human mind. It consists essentially in an economic interpretation of History much more dangerous than that of Marx. That of Marx is dangerous, as Mr. G. K. Chesterton has observed, because: " The theory of all history as a search for food makes the masses content with having food and physic, but not freedom." Instead of the word " freedom," which is vague, I prefer to say participation in the government. But the problem does not consist in the fact that the masses may interpret History economically ; but that a few individuals, or one social class, have taken possession of the means of production, thus creating capitalism, and consequently, the proletariat. Of these individuals and of this class it may indeed be said that they, acted on an economic motive.

This dualism of capital and labour has brought about a world in which the masses have had to interpret History economically, for their material insecurity has made them regard their daily, bread as the highest value. But the economic interpretation of History by, the rich is no longer passive, as in the case of the poor, but active; it is not an effect, but a cause; it is not necessary, but accidental. What is it in substance? It is what all romanticism is: a theoretical justification of our two fundamental sins: lust and pride. And from this theoretical justification has arisen the present world, in which sins have ceased to appear to us to be sins—a fact which does not mean that we can escape their inevitable consequences.

There was a time when men did not contemplate themselves as the centre of the world but as creatures destined to serve their Creator. But men at that time knew themselves to be sinners, and capable, as such, of giving themselves up to lust and pride. On that account laws were passed prohibiting usury, and while these laws remained in force capitalism was impossible. The economic interpretation of history was then a sin in theory and a crime in practice. But the Renaissance came, and with the Renaissance Humanism; and man proclaimed, with Lord Bacon, his own kingdom. He became again the measure of things. There is nothing more interesting in this connection than that passage in Nicholas Barbon, the seventeenth-century English economist, who denies that the value of a thing is its utility, and says that the best judge of the value of a thing is the market. Here we see effected the transmutation of values. The value of a thing is no longer the objective value of its utility but the subjective value given to it by the market—that is, the buyer, the caprice of man. Man has ceased to be a creature, to become a measure and an end. And as man likes to accumulate wealth, wealth too becomes a measure and an end. This is the subjectivization of values.

The promises of Humanism have not been kept. The whole Liberalism of Adam Smith is based on the innocent belief that the nature of man is so constituted that good must result from the free play of his activities. That is not the true nature of man. From the economic liberation of man there may result nothing more than a general scramble for wealth, from which, again, there may ultimately spring a universal conflagration such as the present one or even a greater, in which all the higher cultural values may perish. But the humanist idea is already on the point of being overcome. Man is again considered as the bearer of cultural values, which is, in other words, the same mediæval idea. And with that the economic interpretation of History is yielding place to the aspiration of submitting economic activities to moral ends.

BUREAUCRACY AND WAR

As I have already said that Economics is only an aspect of History, I ought not to be misunderstood if I affirm that a sufficient reason for the present war on its material side may be found in the unchecked growth of bureaucracies. By sufficient reason I do not mean the direct or immediate cause of this great change in the world, but the fundamental *condition* which has made it possible. In the well-known instance of the match that led to an explosion in a powder-magazine, which in its turn blew up a neighbouring city, the *cause* was the lighting of the match, but the *sufficient reason* of the magnitude of the catastrophe was the accumulation of explosives in the vicinity of a town. But, of course, the danger implied in the growth of bureaucracies is a *fact* of another kind than the danger in the accumulation of explosives. The latter danger is a physical fact ; the former, an historical. But as it is a fact common to almost all countries we believe it to be the condition, the general or collective historical sufficient reason of the war.

The cause of this war is not hidden in profound mysteries. The reader already knows enough about it. When Austria prepared to invade Serbia, Russia refused to tolerate it ; Germany sprang to the defence of Austria, declared war on Russia and France, and began her invasion of Belgium, thereby bringing about the intervention of England and giving a pretext for that of Japan. There is no need to look for any other cause, as Mr. Bernard Shaw has done, attributing the war to the Machiavellism of Mr. Asquith and Sir Edward Grey, whom he depicts as astute Jingoes who meditated for years their plan of warring against Germany, but concealed it in order to deceive Germany into believing that England would remain neutral in a European war. But, even if Mr. Asquith and Sir Edward Grey had been as innocent as lambs, England would still have taken up arms to defend the treaty safeguarding the neutrality of Belgium—not from a pedantic love of treaties, but lest the possession of the Belgian coast should promote the naval power of Germany and endanger British independence and the British Empire. Mr. Shaw's hypothesis—ingenious, as we might expect from him, but not very different from that which must have inspired the German poet Lissauer to write his silly " Hymn of Hate "—is therefore unnecessary. It is an attempt to explain to us what we had already explained satisfactorily to ourselves.

If we know, however, that the Austrian Ultimatum to Serbia was the direct cause of the explosion, the accumulation of explosives must be sought in the increase of the bureaucracies. At first sight, I know, this proposition will sound extravagant ; and I also know why. It will sound extravagant because the political thought of the last few decades has been so concentrated upon the disputes between capital and labour that it has not considered the problem of bureaucracy as the problem of an automonous social class, with specific interests of its own. Marx regarded the executive power of States as " a committee for managing the common affairs of the bourgeoisie." On the other hand, the " Kathedersozialisten " in Germany and the Fabians in England looked upon officialism as the instrument of Divine Providence for the solution of social problems. In the same way a few Conservatives have favoured the advance of officialdom, if only because it tended to consolidate the supremacy of the classes over the masses. For others, on the contrary, the rise to power of Ministerial departments at the expense of the taxpayer seemed like the approach of the social revolution. What neither party had noticed, but what a few isolated voices had declared here and there to be a fact, was that the supremacy of the bureaucracy was nothing more, primarily and essentially, than the supremacy of the bureaucracy. But neglect of the power of officialdom did not diminish its power, any more than ignorance of the law of gravitation diminished, three centuries ago, its effect on material bodies.

Nevertheless, when we say that the increase of bureaucracies clearly brings with it the necessity for a great international conflict we enunciate a proposition so intrinsically true that we do not need to have recourse to the method of detailed historical investigation to demonstrate its truth, for its truth may be deduced from the very analysis of its terms.

I call all those men officials—soldiers or civilians, priests or judges, engineers, doctors, or clerks—who receive their emoluments from the public funds. From their position itself it is to be inferred that they must form, in every State, the nationalist and patriotic class by antonomasia. For the remaining classes the national idea of a sovereign State is a disinterested, sentimental, and romantic ideal. For the officials, on the other hand, the State is not only an ideal but a source of income. It has been said— by Mr. Norman Angell, I believe—that when the Germans annexed Alsace-Lorraine the rich of

Alsace-Lorraine went on being rich, the poor continued to be poor, labourers were still labourers, and that the war had been useless from an economic point of view. And it is quite possible that war may be useless from the point of view of labourers, workmen, and masters. But the two thousand French professors in both provinces were replaced by two thousand Germans; and the same thing happened with the army officers, the judges, the officials of the public health boards, and so on. From the point of view of the bureaucratic interests the war was not merely not useless, but positively disastrous, for French officialdom and beneficial to the German. A change of flag may not substantially alter the economic regime of a specified district; but what does undoubtedly change is the bureaucratic personnel. The official follows the flag. The official is therefore the permanent soldier of the flag.

It may be objected that the concept of officialdom does not, a priori, disprove the possibility of States uniting in an International Federation, which, Kant dreamed, would one day result in "perpetual peace." But observe that officials are, in every country, the executive power of the State, and therefore the reality of sovereignty, and that no group of men will give up sovereignty so long as they can contrive to maintain it; and we shall begin to doubt, a priori, whether internationalism can arise from conferences such as those held at The Hague; for even if the special class of officials called diplomatists would rather like to become the arbiters of the world, the remaining officials would not allow it. We do not need experience to prove to us that officials are always anxious to extend the power of their own State over other lands, just as they are hostile to giving up in favour of a greater State the sovereignty of their own. It is obvious that when Italy and Germany were achieving their unity the greatest friends of the ideal of unity were the officials of the absorbing States, Prussia and Sardinia ; and the greatest enemies of unity the officials of the States absorbed, i.e. the States of Southern Germany and Italy. We might have saved ourselves this appeal to experience by an analysis of the interest of officialdom.

From this nationalism and imperialism of officials comes their militarism ; and officials are militarists in two senses : First, in aspiring to make the military power of the State the exclusive function, or the almost exclusive function, of the executive ; for, if this power be in the hands of the executive, it is, *ipso facto*, in their own hands, and this makes officials the hereditary enemies of any political system in which the military power does not lie with the executive—as was the case, for instance, with the feudal system. Secondly, officials are militarists in so far as they view with benevolent eyes the increases in military expenditure ; for they see in armed force a guarantee of their security of tenure, and because the existence of an efficient armed force permits them to cherish hopes of the future expansion of their State. It is true that officialdom could obtain the security to which it aspires in a kind of International Federation which would guarantee its privileges ; but then this security would be obtained at the cost of sovereignty, and the sacrifice would be too painful to be made voluntarily. On the other hand, it is indisputable that the civilian classes of the bureaucracy prefer an increase in their own numbers to an increase in the military class. School-teachers, for example, will wish the sums allocated in the Budget to be spent on education rather than on the navy ; and if we suppose that the funds set aside for the bureaucracy are confined to unalterable limits (as when the Church lived on its tithes), it follows that the different categories of officials will struggle with all the greater avidity for the different sums in the Budget. They are still quarrelling over them ; but, in so far as they do not jeopardize their own salaries, officials will always be favourable to increased military charges, since military charges are a guarantee of their actual possessions and even of their hopes, it being granted that the loss of power by a State would ruin its buraucracy, while the conquest of new territory would widen the bases of the official hierarchy and still further elevate its summits.

We thus indicate yet another of the specific characteristics of officials as a social class. It is perhaps the only social class interested positively in the numerical increase of its members. Workmen are not interested in adding to the number of workmen : on the contrary, the larger the number of workmen in the labour market the smaller will be the rate of wages. Neither are peasant proprietors, for with every increase in their number the area apportioned to them correspondingly diminishes. Neither do capitalists ; for, although capitalists do not compete with one another, their different blocks of capital do compete in the market, and an increase in the number of capitalists means either a diminution in the amount of capital possessed by each one of them, or else an increase in the total volume of capital available, and consequently a recrudescence of competition. But officials, on the other hand, are not interested in seeing their total numbers reduced, for neither they themselves nor their salaries, which are fixed, compete with one another. On the contrary, as public officials are a hierarchy, we may lay down

the general principle that the wider the basis of
an official organization the higher will be its peaks,
so that the position of the heads of the judiciary,
of the national defence, of the education department,
etc., will be all the higher in proportion to the
greater number of officials brought into the service ;
and every increase in the personnel of the adminis-
trative categories carries with it, obviously, rapidity
of promotion for employees who entered the service
sooner.   On the other hand, except in the case of
societies inhabiting new countries, whose members
give themselves up to the passion of exploiting un-
explored riches, public functions and offices are
necessarily coveted by an increasing number of
people, as much for the social dignity which their
character gives them as for the fact that officials live
on fixed salaries, far from the world of competition,
and without exploiting one another.   The attraction
of bureaucratic offices, in short, depends on their
guild constitution.

The tendency of the bureaucracy to increase, however, is antagonistic to the interests of the remaining
social classes.   Officials live on public funds, and
these in their turn must be extracted from private
funds.   We can imagine a society in which there are
no private funds, and in which all the economic
functions, both productive and distributive, are
carried out by public officials ; but in such a society
all the members composing it will be public officials.
In assuming the existence of such a society, we shall
have thereby run counter to the supposition on the
basis of which we have been discussing, viz. a society
in which the officials are to be distinguished from
the remaining citizens by their public character.
In a society in which the citizens are divided into
officials and non-officials the production of wealth
will probably commend itself to the interest of

private persons, while the economic action of the officials will consist in distributing wealth or in consuming it in return for chiefly spiritual benefits, such as culture or justice or the defence of the State. Although the private persons in the society may be favourably interested in the multiplication of public services of all kinds, they are not similarly, interested in their increased cost, for this means an increase in taxation. The norm of the taxpayers consists in obtaining the maximum of public services with the minimum of expense. It may therefore be taken for granted a priori that private citizens will at all times oppose increases in the public expenditure.

As private persons form the great majority of the citizens it will be easy for them to make their own interests prevail ; at any rate, if they unite for the purpose. If private citizens united to check officialdom there is no doubt that officialdom would be checked. And it is clear that if private citizens do not unite, if they are divided by antagonistic interests, the occasion will be propitious for an increase in officialdom. In other words, in homogeneous societies the increase in officialdom cannot be very great. On the other hand, in heterogeneous societies, in which the functions productive of wealth are carried on amid a permanent struggle between rich and poor, and the continual exploitation of man by man, officialdom will easily increase—for two reasons : first, the interests of a united official body will be more powerful than the interests of a disunited society ; and, secondly, because, between the two struggling classes, a way will become opened for the idea of conceding to a neutral class—the official class—the greatest possible maximum of moderating power, so that the antagonism of the two classes may be prevented from degenerating

7

into a civil war or a social revolution. And it is probable, indeed, that the rise of officialdom wards off the approach of a social revolution. But it is th. tragedy of human culture that it cannot solve a problem without setting up a new one in its place ; whence it happens that the rise to power of officialdom, while softening the internal asperities of human societies, thrusts them with fatal effect into external struggles and rivalries.

Officialdom, indeed, increases at the expense of the remaining social classes. Economically speaking, officialdom is immediately parasitical, although mediately it may produce wealth. In any case, the rise of officialism is effected at the expense of the other social classes in the State. But the taxpaying capacity of these classes is limited. There may come a stage at which the demands of the officials exceed these limits. Officialdom may then run the risk of the producing classes finding it no longer to their interest to go on producing. They may prefer emigration to working and handing all their earnings over to the fisc, and they will consequently become enemies of the State that exploits them. In this case the sovereignty of the State will be in jeopardy, for it will be threatened by enemies at home as well as by enemies abroad. And as the sovereignty of the State is the supreme interest of the officials, they will have recourse to any measure rather than continue to exploit the citizens of their State to such a degree as to make their position intolerable. When officials are possessed of the antagonistic desires of wishing to increase as a class, and yet of not wishing to exploit the taxpayers beyond tolerable limits, it is clear that their desires can be satisfied only by extending their power over the inhabitants of other countries.

It thus happens, that we find in the conflict between

the officials and the taxpayers one of the prime
motives of colonial expansion. The purely capitalistic explanation of colonial enterprises is insufficient.
Any one who has lived in German university circles
during the last few years will be able to confirm
my statement that the greatest enthusiasts of
colonial expansion in Germany were not the manu-
facturers, but the students. Their admiration and
envy of British power in India were not aroused
by commercial prospects, but by the possibilities of
posts for military and civil bureaucrats. In the
future colonial empire of Germany the students dimly
discerned billets and pensions for hundreds of thousands of German university graduates. Thus the
interest of the bureaucracy in its conflict with the
interest of the taxpayer was bound to impel the
powerful States to the partition of the colonial
lands ; and as soon as there were none left to be
divided the inevitable result was the clash of the
great bureaucracies, which are the great States,
among themselves.

Facts confirm the accuracy of this abstract
reasoning. The expenditure of the French State,
which was £38,000,000 in 1822, had increased by
1910 to £167,500,000. The expenditure of the
German Empire, which in 1874 was £33,600,000,
rose by 1910 to £133,000,000. The increases in
the English Budget will be in the minds of all, and
in the last nine years the reforms inaugurated chiefly
by Mr. Lloyd George have led to the creation of
sixty thousand new public posts. And it should be
noted that the Budgets have increased as much in
autocratic Russia as in semi-autocratic Germany, in
republican France as in constitutional England, in
countries where pacifist ideas prevail as in those
which boast their lust of conquest—to such an extent
that economists who have observed the phenomenon

speak of a " Law of the increasing activities of the State."

I do not believe such a law exists. If it did exist the increase of unproductive officialdom would be inevitable. But it is not inevitable. What has happened is simply that it has not been avoided. It has not been avoided primarily because its gravity could not easily have been foreseen. All that we know even now is that no political régime up to the present time has been able to solve the problem ; for neither autocracy nor parliamentarism has any direct or immediate interest in checking the increase in officialdom. M. Leroy-Beaulieu has quoted figures to show that the Deputies in the French Chamber devote much more energy to placing their friends in the public services, and thus augmenting the national expenditure, than in reducing the general expenses of the State. Hence we may rest assured that the remedy for the trouble will come neither from an autocracy nor from Parliament, but from the organization of the productive social classes for the specific object of " controlling " the expenditure of States.

But this organization of the productive classes implies the resurrection of the guilds, but guilds with a national function. This is the banner which was first raised in England a few years ago by a modest weekly paper called the *New Age*, with its programme of National Guilds. Disdained by the officials of the State and the State Socialists of the Fabian Society because they refuse to regard the State as the universal panacea ; attacked by the Labour Party because they do not hold an exclusively proletarian idea ; and anathematized by the Marxians because they cannot accept an economico-fatalistic interpretation of history, the men of the *New Age* may nevertheless look into the future with tranquil eyes ; for a guild organization of the nation is the only means of warding off the catastrophes to which we are perpetually exposed by the uncontrolled supremacy of the executive power of the State—the only social class which has so far been formed into a guild. And thus, as the men of the Renaissance by turning their eyes towards antiquity prepared the modern era, so may the men of the *New Age*, with their mediæval conception of the Guild, lay well and truly the foundations of the future.

THE FAILURE OF AUTHORITY

By showing that the unchecked increase of bureaucracy in modern States is a sufficient reason for the present war, we have demonstrated the failure of authority as the basis of society. The rise of bureaucracy against capitalism in the last century has played the same part as the rise, in earlier times, of the monarchical power against Feudalism. Authority is established for the sake of order, and so long as it submits to this function, as we submit the police to it, authority is both necessary and harmless—because the whole of society checks the excesses of authority by means of the very necessity for order which gives rise to it. So long as authority has not behind it a predominant power of its own—in other words, so long as authority finds itself in the same position as the police in England, who have no other weapons than the moral support of the mass of citizens—it has to be confined to its proper function of maintaining order. But as soon as we try to found order on the omnipotence of authority, instead of deriving authority from the necessity for order, the result is disorder, because society abandons itself unconditionally to the ambition of individuals who assume the privileges of authority. And as ambition in its essence is unlimited, it will not be satisfied with anything less than the world for a kingdom.

When a society is established on the basis of authority, one of two results must inevitably follow.

Either (1), as has been the case under unenlightened despotism, the authorities are so blind that they do not consent to the development of any other social values, such as science, art, wealth, etc., and that means the impoverishment of the whole of such societies, and, as a result, their ultimate destruction, or (2) the authorities are enlightened, and they devote part of their power to the development of every kind of social value ; and, in this case, enlightened despotism will inevitably tend towards universal monarchy.   The reason for this is that the enlightened despotism will always find itself stronger than unenlightened societies and than all liberal societies, even if the latter happen to be enlightened ; for despotism has in itself a unity of purpose and direction which liberalism must lack. And as a dream of universal monarchy must unite against the would-be monarch the societies menaced, the result will be a universal conflagration such as the present war—a flaming and lasting proof that order based on authority leads and must lead to the greatest disorders.

LIBERTY AND HAPPINESS

LIBERTY AND ORGANIZATION

IF we take our stand on the supposition that the horrors of the present war and the refutation of the German theory of the State must urge European societies to constitute themselves into some kind of syndicalist or guild organization, based on function as the only source of right, what obstacle is likely to be placed in the way of the triumph of this idea? In my opinion, the most serious obstacle is that of the Liberal ideology which accompanies the present syndicalist movement. Liberalism is individualistic by nature. Its ideal is not the balance of power, or, what is the same thing, justice ; but the indefinite expansion of the individual. But this expansion of the individual is, by definition, incompatible with all social discipline. And, if it lack discipline, syndicalism cannot triumph.

The Liberal principle offers, again, no solution to the problem of apathy ; and this is the origin of the anxiety with which some of the noblest souls in England are inquiring whether one of the most popular dogmas of British politics can serve them as a guide in the hour of crisis. It is true that it is not liberty so much as democracy which is being discussed, but this only means that the question has not been properly set forth. In the *British Review* Mr. H. C. O'Neill has asked, " Can democracy be organized ? " and has answered, " No." His reasoning is based on the supposition that the spirit of modern democracy is that of liberty, "although to say this is to make a gigantic assumption." So gigantic, in fact, that it cannot be accepted for a single moment.

That a democracy may be organized is seen in the example of France, where there is scarcely an individual right which has not been sacrificed to the general determination to bring the war to a satisfactory conclusion. In the same number of the *British Review* as that in which Mr. O'Neill writes we may read the text of a recent French law the object of which is : " To prescribe that none shall escape from the sacred obligation of doing for the defence of his country all that his strength will permit him to do. Consequently, it is meant to place at the disposal of the high command the maximum of forces available." Here is an instance of a democracy capable of sacrificing individual selfishness to the common aim. Mr. O'Neill may object that France is not a pure but an imperfect democracy ; but his article does not refer to pure democracies, but to those at present in existence.

Mr. O'Neill's argument rests on the following assertion : " The prime and final effect of democracy seems to be the changing of the centre of gravity in the State from the good of the people to the good of self." But to say this is to forget that democracy does not arise and cannot arise or maintain itself in existence except in the common will. By " common will " I do not mean, like Rousseau, a sort of mystic collective will, but the thing or the things willed or needed in common. A democracy is not and cannot be an aggregate of isolated individuals with no common ends. Every type of society, and not only democracy, has arisen precisely from community of aims. In places where the individuals speak in monologues and act for purely personal ends there is no society at all. Every society is a society for common ends. In autocracies the formulation and carrying out of these ends are entrusted to the monarch ; in aristocracies to a few persons ; and in democracies it is the people who decide. The individuals do not meet together to fulfil purely individual aspirations. My own, for instance, might be to be loved by a woman who does not love me, and to increase my power of sustained thinking by two hours a day. It might perhaps occur to me to confide my troubles to a friend, but it would be absurd to propose that an assembly of men should apply its collective will to them. An assembly of men can apply its will only to subjects which are common beforehand to the individuals taking part in the meeting. Without a previous identity of the thing desired an act of the common will is impossible. Democracy cannot remove the centre of gravity of the State to the individual ego, because the individual part of the ego necessarily remains beyond reach of the State and of the common will. In every man there is at once the solitary and the citizen. The solitary escapes not only the power of the autocrat, but the power of the community as well. The citizen and the city, however, are one and the same thing. The difference between autocracy and democracy is that in the former there is only one citizen who is perennially active, while in a democracy all the citizens are alternately active and passive —active in deciding the thing which ought to be secured by law, and passive in carrying it into effect according to their functions and talents.

To organize is simply to unite men under external rules for the attainment of a common end by means of the division of their labour. This definition

covers the four elements of which every organization
is composed : the common end, the men who unite,
the rules they must obey, and the work allotted to
each man. The value of every organization is the
value of its elements—the importance of the common
end of the men who are organized ; the number
and quality of the men ; the fitness of the rules
for the object it is sought to achieve ; and, finally,
the proper division of labour. Not one of these
elements is influenced by the fact that the Government may be autocratic, oligarchic, or democratic.
There are large and small autocracies as there are
large and small democracies. In Germany the
division of labour is greater than in France, but
that is due to Germany's greater industrial expansion, and not to the German form of government ;
and the aim of the organization to which we have
been referring—National Defence—is identical in
both countries. It may be said that the rules to
which men have to submit are not so strict in
a democracy as in an aristocracy. This is the only
serious objection made to democracy. But it does
not stand the test of analysis. When democracy
organizes itself to carry out an end whose execution
calls for unity of command, the democracy achieves
its object by entrusting its collective strength to
the man who inspires it with confidence for the
execution of this command. Thus it often happens
that the officers of a democracy—a Joffre or an
Abraham Lincoln—may exercise greater authority
than the officers of a monarchy or an oligarchy.
There are two reasons for this : in the first place,
such officers rely upon the active co-operation of
the people which has appointed them to their
positions ; and, in the second place, because they
possess the knowledge that they are carrying into
effect the common will, and this knowledge arouses

in them a determination to make certain that their
object shall be achieved.

A mystic autocrat may fortify his mind with the
belief that God is guiding him, and the authorities
appointed by the autocrat will harden their resolu-
tions in a spirit of loyalty and obedience towards
the sovereign.   The same thing may happen in
oligarchies possessed of the conviction of their
governing mission, and in the authorities appointed
by such oligarchies.   But round about the autocracy,
the oligarchy, and their authorities the masses of
the people will lie like an enormous and mysterious
note of interrogation.   And so an autocracy or an
oligarchy may be tormented by the doubt whether
its will coincides with that of the people, and this
doubt will blunt its resolution.   On the other hand,
the authority appointed by a democracy will not
see in the masses a perplexing interrogation, but
an explicit mandate, the evidence of which makes
the authority inexorable in carrying it out.   The
law must be put into effect which prescribes that
" none shall escape from the sacred obligation of
doing for the defence of the country all that his
strength will permit him to do," and the same
public which affirms this act will transform itself
into an agent of its fulfilment, and help the
authorities to drag from their hiding-places any
embusqués who may be endeavouring to avoid their
duty.

This immense power wielded by the authority
in a democracy is precisely what inspired John
Stuart Mill to write his essay " On Liberty."   Mill's
liberalism was not so much directed to the defence
of the rights of the individual against a tyrant as
against society itself: " There is a limit to the
legitimate interference of collective opinion with
individual independence, and to find that limit and

maintain it against encroachment is as indispensable to the good condition of human affairs as protection against political despotism." And although Mill twice says that the individual " may rightfully be compelled " " to bear his fair share in the common defence "—for Mill was no fool—his essay " On Liberty " and his other works helped to make the strange opinion prevail that the mission of the law and of the State should be limited to seeing that individuals should mutually respect the liberties of one another. To wish to build up society, not on positive solidarities, but upon barriers which prevent the coercion of some individuals by others, is like wishing to establish marriage not on the sacrament, not on love, and not even on mutual obligations, but simply on the principle that the man and wife shall not open one another's letters, shall not ask one another awkward questions, and shall have nothing in common.

It is this principle of individual liberty, and not that of democracy, which is radically and irremediably opposed to all organization, because in any organization the individual can be nothing more than the organ of the thing willed in common. For Liberalism, on the other hand, the isolated individual is the source from which emanates all good, or, at any rate, the supreme good. And let it not be said that Mill's Liberalism is an antiquated thing. A Liberal such as Mr. Hobhouse, who declares himself to be an interventionist and even a Socialist, says in his book on " Liberalism " that " the function of State coercion is to override individual coercion," and in this idea coercion is always an absolute evil, and respect for the individual is the supreme good. There is no need for me to say that coercion is bad when it is used for evil purposes, as, for example, to punish thought, to put difficulties in the way of the production of wealth, and to impede the development of human values, either cultural or vital. Coercion is a good thing, on the other hand, when it sacrifices individual apathy on the altar of national defence or the progress of thought, hygiene, morality, or national wealth. Nor is it a fact that coercion can only be justified as a means to an end, in accordance with the Jesuitical theory. Coercion is not an evil in itself. Coercion implies Power ; it is power ; and power is a good thing—at least an instrumental good.

Mill would have transcended in principle his negative conception of society if he had paid more attention to his own definition of the concept of Progress—" as the preservation of all kinds and amounts of good which already exist and the increase of them . . . for Progress includes Order, but Order does not include Progress." Mill, however, feared lest by progress would be understood nothing more than the idea " to move onwards," the metaphor of the road which Mr. Chesterton has justly deprecated. This led Mill to neglect his own magnificent conception of progress as a criterion of the goodness or badness of societies and organizations. But he was wrong. With his conception of progress he would still have guaranteed all the goods which he believed he was assuring to people by means of liberty,—thought and character—but he would as well have avoided all the evils which individual liberty positively allows, such as indifference, apathy, frivolity, and the misapplication of human energies to such anti-social aims as that of leaving children rich enough to be useless if they please.

8

COMPULSION AND DEMOCRACY

THIS problem of compulsion must be faced courageously by all democrats. In a war in which England is fighting immediately for the balance of power in Europe, but mediately for her very existence, compulsory military service has been introduced. But it has been introduced for the purely military reason that England must make up with her own contingents the numerical deficiency of France, due to the hedonistic ideology which has prevailed there for more than half a century. But, before its expediency, the justice or injustice of compulsion should have been discussed. In other countries compulsion has been maintained by the democratic parties and attacked by the defenders of privilege. But the question is this: Is it just for the most patriotic to sacrifice themselves to defend the interests of those who remain in their homes? And to a question set forth in these terms the answer must be in the negative. It is not just that the good should be sacrificed to the bad. On the contrary, what is just is that the bad should be sacrificed first.

The necessity for dealing with this problem may be seen in the reply made by the *New Statesman*, the organ of State Socialism in England, to a question asked by Sir Leo Chiozza Money, the economist. This is the question:—

" May I respectfully invite you, as the main repository of the Socialist conscience, to give us a leader endeavouring to reconcile the functions of the State, as recognized by Socialists, with your clinging to Voluntaryism in war ? "

And this is the reply: —

" ' Socialist principles ' no more involve compulsory soldiering than they involve compulsory shoeblacking. If the State needs soldiers or shoeblacks, it is absolutely entitled, in our opinion, to call upon its citizens to fulfil those duties, using compulsion if necessary. But if it finds that it can get all the soldiers or shoeblacks that it wants, and get better ones at that, by calling for volunteers, there is nothing in ' Socialist principles ' to hinder it from adopting the simpler, more efficient, and morally superior method. Sir Leo Chiozza Money will no doubt deny that voluntary methods are simpler or more efficient in the present case, but the issue thus raised between us is one of fact and of expediency, not of principle. The only principle involved is the *right* of the State to use compulsion if necessary, and that we have always upheld."

This reply seems to ignore not only the Socialist principle, but every juridical one. According to it, the " right " of the State—I, as a Socialist, prefer to say the " right " of society—to apply compulsion is conditioned by necessity. If compulsion is necessary to enable the State to obtain all the soldiers or shoeblacks it needs, then compulsion is just. If it is not necessary, it is not just, and then it is preferable to adopt the voluntary method, as it is " simpler, more efficient, and morally superior." All this appears to be as plausible at first sight as the appearance that the sun rises in the east and sets in the west. It remains to be seen whether it stands the test of analysis.

The theory of compulsion, in the case we are speaking of, is identical with the theory of law, since every juridical rule is compulsory.; and if it is not compulsory ("enforceable," as the English lawyers say) it is not juridical at all, but merely a "conventional" rule, without legal sanction. But the laying down of a law does not strictly depend upon its being necessary,. There are very few laws which are necessary, for the preservation of society. Generally speaking, if they are useful that is a sufficient *raison d'être* for them. In many cases—for example, the great majority of the laws relating to private rights—the promotion of the laws does not depend upon their serving the interests of society in general, but the interests of the governing classes in particular. In all cases, laws are prescribed to force the individual to respect them. And that is because it has been thought preferable that individuals should be forced to obey the social will than that they should be allowed to frustrate it.

Necessity is not, and cannot be, any criterion of the justice of a law. The German Chancellor appealed to necessity to justify, the invasion of Belgium. Why did the conscience of humanity refuse to heed this appeal of the Imperial Chancellor? Because to the German "necessity" to win the war there was opposed the necessity on the part of Belgium to maintain her independence ; and high above both "necessities" stood the international treaties which expressed the conscience of humanity. The "right" of the "State" to compel its citizens to carry out their duties is independent of necessity. In any, given society there may be, for instance, 10 per cent. of the citizens who do not perform their duties as citizens, without society expressing the least desire that they should do so.

A country may, possess so much accumulated wealth that it does not require the service of these citizens. It may even be pleased to maintain them in idleness, and even to reward their idleness with luxuries. But, at a given moment, without the country becoming poorer, or really needing the services of these idle people, the public conscience may change and say, for purely moral reasons, that it is not well that their state of idleness should continue. The public may then take measures which, directly or indirectly, will compel the idlers to work. Shall it then be said that such measures are not just because they are not strictly, necessary?

The part played by. necessity in the formation of new laws is that of a driving force. Laws whose substance does not affect more than a restricted number of individuals may be accepted by. the people at large without any pressure on the part of necessity, but merely for the sake of the convenience of some and by the passive consent of the rest. But the revolutionary laws, such as that of universal service or industrial conscription, laws prejudicial to a large number of vested interests, could be promulgated and enforced only when the public conscience was convinced of their "necessity," for without the pressure of necessity such laws would never come into operation. A just idea, but one of a revolutionary character affecting great interests, can acquire active legal status only when necessity renders it "expedient." But its justice depends, not on its expediency or necessity, but on its adjusting itself to ethical ideas.

A law of industrial conscription would be unjust if it were not universally applicable, so far as both persons and things are concerned. It would not be just to compel the poor to work ten hours a day at the manufacture of shells if the rich were not likewise called upon to do their share. Nor would it be just for industrial conscripts to work for fixed salaries or wages if the employers continued to manage their business for their own personal profit. I have read that this is being done in Germany, where the Government, thanks to its system of compulsory service, has been able to send thousands of soldiers to work in the fields or in the factories where war munitions are being made. These men work for half or a third of their normal wages, since they are subject to military law and are afraid to resist lest they should be sent to the front, while their employers are nevertheless getting wealthier—nominally, at any rate—through their Government contracts. This only proves that the governing classes in Germany are quite as unjust towards their own people as they are towards the Belgians, and that they are not only unworthy to govern other countries, but are not even fitted to administer their own.

On the other hand, universal compulsion that has for its object making all citizens fulfil the functions which society deems necessary, is not only just, but it is the very definition of a social régime founded on justice. Such compulsion as this may be too revolutionary to be applied in a day, or two with any hope of success. It does not matter. It is the duty of us all to forward the day when this compulsion shall be applied, not merely in war but in peace. For this compulsion is nothing but the realization of the Socialistic ideal which allows nobody to enjoy the advantages of society without performing one of the functions which society declares necessary. According to the voluntary principle, a man is absolved from any social function if he is financially independent, or if he can find somebody who will support him for nothing. But this right is emphatically denied both by State Socialists and Guild Socialists. The duties of citizens are compulsory in Socialism. The question of the method by which compulsion should be applied is secondary. It is not necessary to set a policeman behind every citizen to make him do his duty. It is sufficient to withhold social assistance from him (food, clothing, shelter, etc.) if he refuses to do it. This is being done already where the poor are concerned. But we Socialists want this compulsion to be extended to the wealthy ; and the best means for applying it to them, we think, is to make the community the inheritor of their wealth. Our principle is compulsion all round.

As we have already identified economic power with military power, it is obvious that military service is a function to secure an economic or instrumental value. Therefore, the question of the existence or non-existence of an organization devoted to national defence ought to be determined by the criterion of necessity or expediency. By this very criterion must be fixed the quantity of social power which has to be devoted to this service. It would be absurd, for instance, if, for the sake of a so-called moral expediency, a million soldiers were maintained where a hundred thousand would be enough to secure the defence of a country. But the question of recruiting the soldiers is no longer a question of expediency but of justice. There is an essential difference between recruiting soldiers and recruiting shoeblacks, and this essential difference explains that it is just that military service should be compulsory, while another service, such as shoe-blacking, should not be. It won't do to reply that this difference consists in the fact that more soldiers are wanted than shoeblacks. That is a quantitative answer to a question of qualities.

Neither more nor less nor expediency can be criteria of justice. The reason is a different one. The service of a shoeblack is purely professional. And the professions of men ought to be determined not only by social necessity but by the fitness of the individual. The principle of social necessity requires that every individual shall fulfil one of the functions necessary for the maintenance of society. That of fitness demands that the vocation should be respected, provided that this vocation is not that of idleness. There is also a professional side to military service, which consists in the knowledge of the different techniques of war. In this professional side the voluntary principle must be respected as far as possible. But there is also a non-professional side, which consists in submission to discipline and the risking of life. The vocation here is no longer professional, but heroic. And it is not just to sacrifice the heroes alone. It is more just to sacrifice those who are not heroes, although this may be inexpedient from a strictly military point of view.

What a Socialist cannot say is that the voluntary recruiting of soldiers is morally superior to the compulsory. It would be more moral only if all men —absolutely every, man—fulfilled their obligations towards society by a spontaneous impulse. If a single man failed to do his duty, that fact would morally justify the passing of a law making it obligatory on him to do it. It is not at all moral for the more patriotic to do their duty and for the less patriotic to fail to do so. It would not be moral, again, if the Treasury were able to cover its expenditure by voluntary donations, and if, in such a case, generous men were to ruin themselves while the avaricious continued to accumulate wealth. Laws have been passed to prevent this kind of

immorality by compulsory means ; and it is useless
to say that laws cannot compel the unwilling people
to work, as they will have recourse to passive resistance.   The whole experience of mankind proves
the contrary.   To deny that compulsion is efficacious
is to deny the efficacy of all the laws ever made,
just or unjust.   " Superior " morality is lacking
in the voluntary method because it is not superior
that I, an individual, do my duty.—for that is
·" elementary " ;   I ought to vote as well for a
law to make my neighbour fulfil his obligations,
and I ought further to help the police when they
have to arrest my neighbour for not doing what
he is obliged to do.

Socialism must be, by definition, much more
legalist or compulsory than individualism.   Socialism
holds that every society must regulate the functions
necessary for its maintenance :   (a) the army, (b)
shoeblacks, (c) art, (d) agriculture, etc., and compel every man to exercise the function for which
he shows the greatest aptitude ;   reserving to itself
the right to change the function when a change
is shown in the aptitude.   For the fulfilment of his
service the man receives pay according to his
function, and if he discharges no function he
receives no pay.   If the individual refuses to help
society, society in its turn will refuse to help the
individual, who will consequently die of hunger :
the same in State Socialism, if it is really Socialism,
as in Guild Socialism.   Under Guild Socialism the
Guild allots to the man the duties for which he
appears to be best fitted.   That seems to me better
than State Socialism, for only shoemakers can tell
whether another shoemaker is good or bad.   But
the Shoemakers' Guild would take care to see that
every shoemaker earned the pay assigned to him
by the Guild.   And the other Guilds would take

care, for their part, that the Shoemakers' Guild did not obtain more products than justly corresponded to its work. Disputes between the Guilds would be fought out in open court, as at present. And the judgments of the courts would be compulsory, as now. And by saying all this I simply mean that progress in Socialization is likewise progress in compulsion—in just compulsion.

What I do not say is that all forms of compulsion are just, nor are all laws just. There are just and unjust laws. The fact that a law regulates a necessary social function does not imply that the law is just. It may be expedient, from a purely national point of view ; but if unjust, it means, like every unjust expedient, bread for to-day and hunger for to-morrow. It may apparently save the situation at a critical moment, but in reality it will corrupt and destroy a society which seeks to prolong its life by means of unjust expedients. Absolute justice would demand the universal mobilization (or socialization) of all the resources of a country—men, women, capital, land, tools—for the common cause ; and the common cause, in time of war as in times of peace, is the preservation and enrichment of spiritual and material values.

As for the necessity of compulsion, let me point out that, as culture and thought penetrate the popular classes, there is an increase in the number of individuals who are aware not only of what they think and will, but of being themselves the agents of thought and will. This consciousness of ourselves is self-consciousness. And when we add to this feeling of self-consciousness a judgment of positive valuation, the self-consciousness becomes personality ; and we appreciate in personality a unique irreplaceable good, which ought not to be destroyed or endangered. The consciousness of personality is the apple that Adam and Eve ate in the Garden of Eden. This consciousness of personality is the basis of the original sin, although the Renaissance tried to make a virtue of it. Why? Because the more powerful in us the feeling of personality becomes, the more difficult is it to induce men to risk their personality to defend their country, and the more difficult, also, is it to induce women to run the risks involved in the bearing and bringing up of children. This difficulty will increase with the progress of education to such a degree that, unless the world suddenly rediscovers the meaning of religion, the hour is approaching in which civilized societies will not be able to ensure their existence if they do not supplement compulsory military service for men by compulsory maternity for women.

LIBERTY AND THOUGHT

It is obvious that compulsion attacks personal liberty. But why, should personal liberty be sacred? It was to this problem that Stuart Mill devoted his essay "On Liberty." He solved it by saying that personal liberty is sacred because it favours the progress of thought. If the answer were true, personal liberty would have to be respected; for, in fact, the progress of thought—that is, the acquisition of new truths and the maintenance of those already known—is really, an absolute value, an end in itself. But is it true that personal liberty favours the intellectual progress of a country?

The question may be stated thus: Which is better for the progress, development, and advancement of thought in a country—liberty, of thought or the organization of thinking? The problem has recently become actual in the discussions concerning the urgency of organizing thought in England for the purpose of the war. In a speech by Lord Haldane we find these phrases:—

"Since 1898 I had been engaged in a campaign of education, and that campaign was only typical of the extraordinary difficulties which everybody had to encounter who tried to waken this nation before it chose to be wakened to the business of organizing itself. . . . We must beware of our easy-going habit as a nation. We were too prone to assume that everything was all right. What we wanted was a spirit of observation and question.

. . . The nation must organize. Men and women must fit themselves to learn and think and act as they had never thought of acting before. Then it might be that the war and the convulsion which had awakened us out of our slumbers might prove to have been a blessing. We needed, in the lethargy into which we had got, an intellectual and spiritual awakening."

It is obvious that in order to solve the technical problems raised by the war the organization of thought is indispensable. Individual initiative may enable a small body of soldiers to escape the effects of asphyxiating gas by the simple device of climbing a tree if one be near ; but it is for the expert to provide the Army with the best possible respirators. And what applies to gas may be extended to Zeppelins, barbed wire, the big howitzers, the enormous numbers of machine-guns, to submarines, and every problem of the war. The possession of a great number of inventive minds would not be of much use to a country if they were not organized in such a way as to be able to apply their talents on a big scale to the military needs. But military needs do not differ in kind, they only differ in urgency, from the needs of peace. Industrial supremacy can only be maintained by the constant invention of new industrial processes and by the constant adaptation of industry to them. The inventions may emanate from isolated minds, although they are more frequent in countries where the work of research in laboratories is better organized. But the adaptation of industries to inventions demands an intimate connection between industrial production and the work of research. The investigator must concentrate himself not upon his own whims, but on the problems set by the industries that pay him for his investigations. The industrial owners, in their turn, must follow closely the progress of science, since on it depends the growth or decay of their business. Note the close relationship between the rise of the chemical industry in Germany and the employment of some thirty thousand chemists in the work of industrial research at an average cost of £200 a year each.

All this is obvious, as I say, and I should be ashamed to repeat it if several of the most eminent thinkers had not spent considerable energy in trying to prove that the best way to promote thinking is to maintain liberty of thought. Stuart Mill, for instance, in his " Principles of Political Economy," defends private property against communist systems on the ground that " it is compatible with a far greater degree of personal liberty." But in his Essay on Liberty he bases the principle of personal liberty on the fact that it ensures the progress of human thought. " The central idea of the ' Liberty ' is the immense importance to mankind of encouraging and promoting a large variety of types of character and modes of thinking, thus giving full freedom to human nature to expand and improve in all kinds of directions," says Mrs. Fawcett in her Introduction to the Essay. Stuart Mill has his eye upon the sage like Socrates or Christ maintaining his own opinion on matters of religion and ethics against a hostile world, and writes the well-known lines : " If all mankind minus one were of one opinion, and only one person were of the contrary opinion, mankind would be no more justified in silencing that one person than he, if he had the power, would be justified in silencing mankind."

The problem of Mill was primarily that of the powerful thinker fighting against an obscurantist authority seeking to crush his ideas by force. The solution that Mill sought for this problem was to secure for such a thinker by political liberty the liberty of thought. But in the course of his Essay he discards the solitary thinker and fixes his mind on the intellectual development of the masses, and says :—

" Not that it is solely, or chiefly, to form great thinkers, that freedom of thinking is required. On the contrary, it is as much, and even more, indispensable to enable average human beings to attain the mental stature which they are capable of. There have been, and may again be, great individual thinkers, in a general atmosphere of mental slavery. But there never has been, nor ever will be, in that atmosphere an intellectually active people. Where any people has made a temporary approach to such a character it has been because the dread of heterodox speculation was for a time suspended."

Here one can see plainly the central error of Stuart Mill's liberalism. Great thinkers are not made by liberty of thinking, but merely by thinking even " in a general atmosphere of mental slavery," and the interest of the masses of the people in the discussions of thinkers is not to be attained by the non-intervention of the temporal powers in matters of thought, but, on the contrary, through the mutual intervention of the actual powers of society in the labours of thinkers, and of thinkers in those questions of the distribution of power which always awaken the interest of the masses.

Liberty of thinking is a very equivocal concept. It may mean, as it meant in Stuart Mill, the acknowledgment of the utility of discussion for the progress of thought, and in such a case I am also a liberal, as I certainly believe in the efficacy of the dialectical method and in the utility of the " devil's advocate," whose arguments are patiently listened to by the

Roman Catholic Church at the canonization of a saint. In the French army there is a wonderful institution called " *la critique*." In the periods of instruction, inspection, and manœuvre the commander of every movement, even of small units like a platoon, is called upon to justify it before his inferiors by replying to the questions of his superiors. Here we can see in practice the principle of discussion without the principle of liberty. Discussion has ceased to be a right, and has become a function and a duty.

But you have only to look at a newspaper stall or even at a bookseller's window, and think of the scanty value of the huge amount of printed matter, to realize that liberty of thinking, or, rather, liberty of printing, may only mean indifference to thought and the rising of that " vague, shapeless, ubiquitous, invulnerable Thing " called the Great Boyg, which Ibsen introduces in " Peer Gynt " to symbolize the dull resistance of inertia to the advance of thought. And when " the Great Boyg conquers, but does not fight," shall the thinkers refuse the help of the temporal powers to remove mental laziness, even by compulsion, if necessary? Government interference may be very bad, if against thought, but very good if in its favour.

Against this proposition was written Buckle's " History of Civilization in England." With the first part of this thesis, " that the progress of society depends on intellect," we can safely agree ; but Buckle asserted, too, that the " protection " exercised by Governments, the nobility, the Church, etc., over thought has dwarfed and held back the cause of freedom and civilization. He even said that " to protect literature is to injure it." English literature was strong because it " had been left to develop itself. William of Orange was foreign to it ; Anne cared not for it ; the first George knew no English, the second not much."

It is true that during the eighteenth and the nineteenth centuries the kings of England did not care much for the progress of thought, but it was not so in the preceding two hundred years. Henry VII, " a wonder for wise men " (Bacon), was a patron of scholarship. Henry VIII possessed a culture vastly superior to that of his two great rivals, Francis I and Charles V, and his accession to the throne was hailed by Erasmus and More as the crowning triumph of the Renaissance. Queen Elizabeth could read Greek, Latin, French, and German ; James I was a scholar, Charles I a divine ; Charles II, the founder of the Royal Society, an adept of physical philosophy. No other country in the world has had the fortune of being governed during six generations, the one after the other, by scholarly monarchs. And as the nobility replaced the power of the Crown, they took also in charge the patronage of learning. And to-day it is the State that is the great promoter of education and research. For thought is not a spontaneous product of liberty ; the thinking of the world is, as a rule, done by professors who think by duty and not only by right, and the culture of the masses depends on compulsory education, not on freedom.

Both Stuart Mill and Buckle believed that liberty was enough to promote thought. Hence the fervour of their Liberalism. This belief of theirs must have been based on another : on the belief that it was sufficient to permit individuals to think as they wished in order that truths might come spontaneously out of the heads of men. But they do not. And they do not because thought is only a spontaneous activity in thinkers by vocation. The vast majority of men hardly ever think. As a

9

rule a man only thinks when he is in trouble.
During the rest of his life he either dreams or lets
his ideas come together by chance. To concentrate
on objective problems is something done spontaneously only by a handful of men in each generation.
If there were in the world no other intellectual
activity than the spontaneous, this would not
even be enough to preserve actual knowledge, not
to mention the increase of it. That is why Governments, except the very primitive ones, have at all
times devoted a great part of their power to
promoting thought, and even punishing ignorance,
as they punish it in the laws providing for
compulsory attendance at school. It is true that
at other times Governments have devoted their
power to crushing thought. But in that they were
wrong. To employ power in promoting thought
is good ; to employ it in crushing thought is
bad.

Possibly the first man who connected in a relation of cause and effect the two concepts of political
freedom and thought was David Hume, in his essay,
" Of the Rise and Progress of the Arts and
Sciences." In it he says, " *that it is impossible
for the arts and sciences to arise, at first, among
any people, unless that people enjoy the blessings
of a free government.*" Free government means
in this essay the antithesis to absolute monarchical
government. Hume was probably thinking of
Athens and Florence, the two Republics where
government could not be absolute on account of the
very strength of their opposing political parties :
aristocracy and democracy, *popolo grasso* and *popolo
minuto*. This rivalry, of course, is favourable to
the inception of political thought, as it provides
it with polemical grounds. But the execution of
Socrates and Savonarola is enough to prove that

nothing similar to our present liberty of opinion was known in the two cradles of European thought.

The prophet of modern science did not leave to the chance of political happenings the promotion of thought. Bacon wanted protection for research, and better the protection of kings than that of mere noblemen. In his " Advancement of Learning," dedicated to King James, are to be found the principles of the organization of mental activities, whose working in modern Germany is so justly admired by Lord Haldane :—

" Let this ground, therefore, be laid, that all works are overcommon by amplitude of reward, by soundness of direction, and by the conjunction of labours. The first multiplieth endeavour, the second preventeth error, and the third supplieth the frailty of man. But the principal of these is direction. . . ."

We may safely agree with Lord Bacon and let it be said against Buckle that thinking grows with the protection of the governing classes—Churchmen or Kings, landowners, capitalists, or trade unions— and that thinking decays when the governing classes are afraid of talented people or are not intelligent enough to know them when they meet them. Rather a melancholy conclusion, for it has not been found a recipe to secure intelligence in the people with power !

Thought is not only a social function, but one of the most important. If it is a function, like that of railway services, it ought to be acknowledged and organized. A democracy which does not recognize the value of thought will be a democracy either without thought or of an irregular and inefficient thought. It will be an inferior society, like any other, oligarchy or autocracy, which does not acknowledge it.

BEYOND THE BARRIERS OF LIBERTY AND AUTHORITY

I HAVE ventured to assert that the Liberal conception of society is purely or principally negative, since it seeks to raise barriers which hinder the intervention of society in the sphere of individuals. But as negative as the Liberal conception is the authoritarian conception, which sanctifies the ruler and raises him above the wills of the citizens. In speaking thus we have shown the existence of a logical identity between the Liberal and the authoritarian conceptions. Both are conceptions of sovereignty. The individual is the sovereign in the Liberal conception, and the authority is a mere delegation which can be recalled at the will of the individuals. In the authoritarian conception of society, authority is the sovereign by divine right. At bottom, both conceptions take care, above all, to erect barriers of fortresses within which the will of the sovereign is absolute.

Why this identity in the Liberal and authoritarian conceptions? Because both political ideas are founded upon the same type of morality ; a subjective and androlatric morality. Every political idea is based on a moral idea : " Law defines existing legal rights ; ethics defines moral rights ; politics defines those moral rights which would be legally enforceable if the law were what it ought to be,[1]" wrote Mr. Jethro Brown in felicitous words. A subjective morality is that which affirms that

things are good or bad simply because there is
somebody who thinks them or feels them to be
good or bad. And I say that this morality is
androlatric, because even those thinkers who say
that the subject of this morality is not the empiric
man, " the average sensual man," but a thing called
" Reason " or " Practical Reason " (Kant), or
" Pure Will " (Cohen), or the " Universal Spirit "
(Hegel), or " God " (the Jews, Mohammedans, and
Christians), always acknowledge that it is man—
whether as an isolated being, or in the State, or
in authority, or in his own name, or, by Divine
grace, in the name of that entity—who causes things
to be good or bad by the simple fact that he
believes or feels them to be good or bad.

From this subjective morality there must likewise
be derived a subjective politics which tends to
maintain intact the sovereignty of the moral person ;
for the moral person is all the morality which it
is necessary to ensure in the life of the community.
Stuart Mill and the Liberals will say that this moral
person, the fount of all morality, is the individual,
and they devise a system of barricades to render
him inviolate. Hegel and the Germans, generally
speaking, will say that this person is the State
itself, and they, too, will declare the State to be
inviolable, infallible, and Divine. For the authoritarians in the Latin countries this person is God
and His representatives on earth, the Pope on the
one hand and the Monarch on the other ; and
they likewise will wish to raise barriers placing
these persons beyond the reach of criticism. What
is common to all these different political schools
is the fact that they have a positive conception only
of the person or human agent. They all confine
morality to the person and define the good as the
self-realization of the ego—whether this ego is the

man in the street, as in Mill ; the head of the State, as in Hegel ; humanity, as in Kant and Cohen ; or God and His representatives on earth, as in the older authoritarians.

On the other hand, it cannot be said that these schools have a positive conception of society. So far as the Liberals are concerned, society does not really exist. They see in it only a multiplication of their own ego ; but it is obvious that isolated individuals cannot succeed in building up a society, which means continuity and not merely discretion. For the authoritarians, on the other hand, there cannot, properly speaking, be said to be any society either. Their society is nothing but an extension of the autocratic ego which imposes itself upon and dominates the subjects. All that interests the authoritarians and the Liberals is that nothing shall be allowed to touch the inviolability of their favourite subject. They are the angels placed by God in the Eastern Gate of Eden, armed with swords of fire, to prevent Adam and Eve from walking in the path leading to the Tree of Life.

Never in the whole world has there been a purely Liberal society, any more than there has been a purely authoritarian society ; for both the Liberal and the authoritarian principles are nothing but the protective barriers of the autonomy of the individual or of authority ; and society itself is not a barrier, but the common life which spreads above and below and through the interstices of any barriers we may raise. But wherever either principle has prevailed, whether it be the Liberal or the authoritarian, it has prevailed at the expense of the positive content of the social life. Russia and Spain are instances of what the authoritarian principle costs. In those countries the laws tend chiefly to impose a negative system of things by virtue of which no one can invade the sphere of the autocrat. All that a Spanish priest asks of his faithful flock is that they shall not read Liberal publications. And there are many people, indeed, who do not read them ; but there are very few who have the least idea of what Christianity means. For centuries the chief object of the laws passed in Russia was to ensure the avoidance of any discussion of the authority of the Tsar and of the Orthodox Church, though this state of things began to be changed some ten years ago. On the other hand, no great attention has been paid to the positive function of promoting the increase of human values, and especially of cultural values.

The Anglo-Saxon countries, on the other hand, are an example of what the Liberal principle costs. In them the laws take care that, above all else, the individual's sphere of action is not interfered with. The application of the *laissez-faire* principle to industry led to the horrors of the factories in the first half of the last century, when even children were compelled to work, and pauperism became intensified as the increasing use of machinery left men unemployed. The abolition of the older restrictions led, as had been expected, to an increase in production ; but at the same time it concentrated wealth in the hands of a social class which, by virtue of the Liberal principle, was not called upon to fulfil any other social function than that of accumulating dividends. You may tell me that this economic Liberalism was surpassed by Stuart Mill himself when he spiritualized the Liberal principle, and turned it not into an external liberty of action which would enable the most clever or best-situated people to enrich themselves, but into a free play of spiritual originality which was to result in " individual vigour and manifold

diversity." Only, as freedom of thought could be
also interpreted as the right *not* to think, or to
think without logic, its result has not been
"individual vigour " exactly, but the triumph of
the Yellow Press and of a literature which has
tended to benumb the mind.

If the evil has not been greater than it is, this
is simply due to the fact that the subjective
morality from which both the authoritarian and the
Liberal principles are derived has never succeeded in
exercising its authority over the entire human mind.
Men never believed that things were either good
or bad simply because some person believed or
felt them to be so. When we look critically at
the houses in a street and say that some are good
and others bad, we do not merely think that we
believe so, but that the houses themselves are good
or bad. This point has been convincingly demonstrated by the Cambridge thinker, Mr. G. E. Moore,
in his books on " Ethics." But from this ethics
—which is, at bottom, only a scientific formulation
of current morality—there arise, in my judgment,
consequences of political application which will
lead us definitely beyond all the existing subjective
conceptions, both Liberal and authoritarian. I mean
this : when we judge things we judge them in
relation to man, or by a human value. Some houses
are good because they satisfy our economic needs
or our æsthetic taste ; others are bad because they
do not satisfy these exigencies. But, in turn, our
judgments with respect to men are not referred
to themselves, but to the things which they have
produced or may produce. Thus, if we say, as
a regiment of soldiers passes, that the physique
of some men is better than the physique of others,
we are not referring to the value which the body
of each one may have for its possessor, but to

something which appears to us to be good—as, for example, the hardships which a strong man can bear in war better than a man of inferior strength.

In this connection we are assuming that ethics, as the theory of moral values, is only a part of philosophy, conceived as the science of values in general, cultural or vital. But what is more important is not the accordance of our own ideas with that of a particular school of thought, even if this school is gradually winning the assent of the cultural world, but the accordance of this objective foundation of morality with the general practice of common humanity. For always acts of virtue have been preferred before the instruments of it, and a fair judgment of persons cannot be got directly, but only indirectly, through their actions. What Hegel said about nations ought to be said about persons. "What their actions are, that are the persons." It is because there are things possessed of intrinsic value, or useful, that we say that men who maintain them or increase them are themselves good. They may be bad in their hearts, but only God can read in the human heart ; we men cannot judge other men soundly but through their actions.

But in doing so we have carried over the centre of ethics to a point beyond man. The object of morality is no longer the " self-realization of man," whatever is implied in that phrase, but precisely " the preservation of all kinds and amounts of good which already exist and the increase of them." In these very words Stuart Mill defined Progress, but he did really something more. For his progress is the criterion of the value of every society. The good things are heroism and science and art and justice and health and manners and personal beauty and life and power. To maintain them and to increase them—that is absolute good ; to destroy them—that is absolute evil. To increase the lesser goods when it is possible to multiply the greater—that is relative evil. But the important thing is that we have transcended man as the centre of ethics. And so we do in our common life. The day on which we read of the bombardment of Rheims Cathedral by the Germans we felt more aggrieved than if the victims of the shells had been men. And if we had to choose in a shipwreck between saving the " Gioconda," by Da Vinci, or a fellow-passenger, most of us would prefer the " Gioconda." The " Gioconda " is a value to the whole of humanity ; the fellow-passenger may be of value only to his family or to himself.

We do not deny, of course, that there is a relation between goods or moral things and men. We simply assert that this relation is reciprocal. We judge men in their relation with the goods ; and we judge the goods for their value to men. Of a thing whose intrinsic value or usefulness cannot be discovered by men we say that it is valueless. If a man does not increase the existing goods nor even maintain them, we say the same. In this morality men and goods are alternately means and ends. And this morality is the real foundation of every kind of society. For what is the common characteristic of all societies, be they States, limited companies, or football clubs? That men are associated for a common object, and that the fulfilment of this common object is considered superior to the individual aims of its members. So we can say that every society is a society in a common object. Its centre of gravity lies in the object ; its members are purely the organs of the object. It is only because there is a thing which several men find good that associations between men are possible. Men do not associate themselves without something in which they find that their aims are common. A subjective morality cannot give rise to a society because it cannot result but in a multiplication of our own ego or in an expansion of the ego in authority. Society —real society—can only begin when it has been founded on a common end in which individual interests are both transcended and united.

But in the same way as subjective politics are only the consequence of subjective ethics, on objective ethics it is possible to found a system of objective politics. Since men are associated in things, and since they only fulfil their duty when they occupy themselves in the conservation and increase of cultural and vital values, according to schemes of balance and mutual adjustment of the values themselves, the art of politics ought to devote itself to finding the means to make legally enforceable the maintenance and the promotion of cultural and vital goods. With subjective morality disappear, too, subjective rights. Nobody, either King or taxpayer, has more subjective rights than any other person. The legality or legal enforcement of the commands of a man with power should depend no longer upon any kind of personal right, but on the social function legally exercised by him. There would be no longer any personal rights, but the very conception of right would be inextricably united with function, as the idea of morality is inseparable from that of the goods. Where there is no function there would be no rights. The functions would consist, of course, in the maintenance and promotion of the goods. And in this society we should not discuss any longer the rights of the individual or the rights of the Sovereign, for in this society nobody would have any right other than that of doing his duty.

THE IDEAL OF HAPPINESS

WE have already pointed out the juridical formula of a society constituted according to the principles of justice. A society will be just in which social power—economic, military, and political—is distributed according to the functions of the individuals, in which the functions are proportioned to capacities, and in which capacities have an opportunity of developing according to the potentialities of each one. This is the ideal of all the Socialist parties. But before the Socialist parties decide to fight for justice they must revise their tables of values. The present ideology of labour parties is the same as that prevailing among the middle classes. According to this ideology, men can be happy if only their hours of work are shortened, if they can work at what they like, and if the reward for their efforts is increased. Almost all modern books in which Socialistic Utopias are described do nothing more than present visions of abundance to the eyes of the needy. Thus the supreme ideal is that of welfare : " The greatest happiness of the greatest number." And that is not right. These Utopias may please the masses, since the masses are needy ; but they cannot inspire them. A man who does not feel an ideal higher than that of welfare will never risk his life for an idea of justice, for the simple reason that the good which he exposes—his own life—will always be higher than that which he proposes to win—welfare. But if men do not decide to risk their lives, they will never suc-

ceed in abolishing the privileges which perpetuate
social injustice. Thus hedonism and utilitarianism,
which the Labour parties, and especially their
leaders, have learnt from the principles of the
Liberal parties, from the life of the middle classes,
and from the ideals of modern art, have turned
themselves into the chains that bind the workmen to
their present position. A few men may be able to
satisfy their utilitarian ideal even under an unjust
social régime. But the masses will never be able to
satisfy it except under a régime of justice. Justice
will not triumph by itself alone ; in order to triumph
it must have soldiers to fight for it. But the ideal
of utility cannot make good soldiers. And, therefore, the soldiers of justice will have to be men
who may be fond of every kind of comfort, but who
must have overcome the utilitarian morality.

* * *

The reading of a journalist who aims at expressing the meaning of the actualities of collective life
cannot be principally " literary." My own is confined almost entirely to newspapers, which give me
the facts ; to books of science and history, which
enable me to understand them ; and to the classics,
which suggest to me the ideal standards by which
they may be valued. But once or twice a year I read
a novel, too—one of those novels, as a rule, which
after ten or twenty years of criticism, have been
acknowledged to be good. In doing this I find two
kinds of satisfaction. The first consists in feeling, as
I almost invariably do, that my own judgment is in
agreement with that of the authorities of my profession. What my Guild has called good seems good to
me likewise. This reconciles me with the world and
with my own work. A writer, when he agrees with
the judgment of the critics, feels the double pleasure

of imagining that the mind of others has not thought
in vain, and, at the same time, he is encouraged by
the hope that his own mind is not thinking in vain
either.   The second satisfaction, and the more important, is that of purification.   Great novels are
purifying in the same sense that Aristotle spoke of
the catharsis of Greek tragedy.   The hero of novels
is not the hero described by the poet, but every one
of his readers.   To the old question, " What is
Hecuba to us ? " the Latins answered, " De te fabula
narratur."   The story applies equally to yourself.
Great novels are purifying because they free the soul
from the delusion of individual happiness.

    This time it was the turn of George Meredith's
" The Egoist."   In the case of a novelist we have
no right to hope that he shall give us some new conception.   The function of bringing forth conceptions
is not that of artists, but of thinkers.   The character
of the hero once postulated, the course of the fable
is obviously fatal.   The story deals with an egoist
who seeks to defend himself against the possible
hostility of the world by means of a rampart of
human beings, whom he bends to his will.   But,
though the egoist has at his command every kind of
resource—name, money, health, talents, and energy
—Sir Willoughby Patterne proves to be a failure.
The people he has bent to his will cease to interest
him ; those who do interest him are the people who
escape from him—precisely as the great tenor is
moved solely by some obscure newspaper which
dares to dissent from the general encomium ; or
as Don Juan was not flattered by the women he
conquered, but was dragged by the heels by the
only woman who fled from him.   All the pleasure
which Sir Willoughby derives from his successes is
cancelled by his failures.   Happiness cannot lie in
the possession of persons or things, for the pleasure

of the possession diminishes with the number of persons or things possessed ; and, on the other hand, pain is increased by the persons or things which resist us, especially in proportion to the certainty we felt of capturing them.   An entire school of economics—the Viennese—was based on this subjective relativity of the value of things.   This was called the *Grenznutzentheorie*, the theory of the limits of utility ; and, although it is false as economics, precisely because it is founded on individualist psychology (and because it is social psychology which really settles the value of things in the market), it is always true considered as individual psychology.   A pound sterling has a certain objective value in the market independently of my psychology ; but its value for me depends upon the position of this pound sterling in the perspective of my possessions—or, in other words, whether the pounds sterling which I have in my possession are few or many.   In this conceptual sense Meredith's novel tells us nothing new.   Its value lies in the wealth of its words, the subtlety of its descriptions, the fluidity of the narrative, the consistency of the scenes and characters—in short, its imaginative veracity ;   for even on the plane of imagination there is truth and falsehood.

Meredith's " Egoist " thus fills the part of " didactic poems in the grand style " and of " cosmogonies of culture," which the philosopher Cohen assigns to novels in his " Æsthetics."   There are many simple-minded egoists who imagine that they can attain happiness if they devote their life to the satisfaction of their selfishness.   This illusion is destroyed in Meredith's book.   But there are also simple-souled altruists and philanthropists who fancy they can attain happiness by leading a life of self-abnegation, forgetting themselves so that they may devote themselves to the service of others. It was for such as these that Cervantes wrote "Don Quixote." Don Quixote does not find happiness in his attempt to redeem the world, but melancholy and disillusion. His generous lance is broken on the hard skin of human egoism ; and, at the moment of dying, Don Quixote turns his eyes to heaven ; the Happy Isles are certainly not to be found in this world. Sir Willoughby Patterne does not find happiness in serving himself. But neither did Don Quixote find it in serving others. Nor do the heroes of D'Annunzio find it in the service of their pleasures ; nor did Madame Bovary find it in the service of her imagination. And Desgrieux found rest for his soul only in the death of Manon Lescaut, the love of his life. All the novels which announce in their last page the happiness of their heroes are necessarily bad, because they are arbitrarily false. They end at the very moment in which begins the interest of the story.

What happens in novels we find also in life itself. When the Athenian magistrates freed Socrates from the fetters which were hurting his leg in prison, the sage began his discourse (" Phædo ") on the immortality of the soul, expressing his wonder at the extraordinary analogy existing between pleasure and pain ; for, though men do not see them arriving at the same time, but coming one after the other, they are both as closely intermingled as if they were links of the same chain—and Socrates feels that the pain caused him by the shackles has now been replaced by an equivalent pleasure. Pain and pleasure are contrary states which mutually beget one another, for they are contained one within the other. They are not, says Socrates, concepts which we postulate as fixed, like the number three, but, like life and death, they are alternations of the same subject. In the case of pleasure and pain the permanent substance is our own sensibility.   And the most terrible and dangerous misfortune, adds Socrates subsequently, is that the soul, " compelled to rejoice or to become sad for some reason, thinks that the origin of the pleasure or pain is something very true and real, although it is far from being so."   The soul, indeed, does not rejoice or repine *through external causes*, but *with the occasion* of external causes.   The true cause of its joy or grief lies in the fact that in those states joy and grief mutually engender themselves.

With the object of curing myself of the delusion of happiness, the idea occurred to me some years ago of devising a pendulum theory of sensibility.   According to this theory the law of sensibility is an automatic succession of joy and pain, independent of circumstances ;   and pain and joy do not come to mean more than the reflection in one's consciousness of the systole and the diastole of the nerves. As much as one suffers, one enjoys—that is the law. The more sensitive, the greater will be our joy and our pain ;   and not only our joy or our pain, but both alternately.   And the way of good is the same as the way of evil ;   the same whether we are rich or poor, glorious or unknown, healthy or ill.   We cannot say whether even death itself can stop the oscillation of the pendulum which bears us from joy to sadness and from sadness to joy.   That there is no joy wholly free from sadness is a fact known to everybody.   But moralistic minds must likewise recognize that there is pleasure in ruin, in hunger, in muscular exhaustion, in the betrayal of a loved woman, in fever, in cold, in dishonour, in crime, in being derided, in the shame of cowardice. There is heaven in hell.   I know it.

From this theory we could deduce a refutation a priori of the popular conception of heaven as an

10

eternal pleasure resort, and hell as a place of ever-
lasting torment.   As sensibility acts by contrast,
pleasure is impossible without pain, and pain without pleasure.   Either we shall preserve our sensibility in the next world or we shall lose it when we
die.   If we keep it we shall go on feeling pleasure
and pain both in hell and in heaven.   This association of the ideas of pleasure and heaven and pain
and hell, however, is not maintained by all theo-
logians.   The wisest of them tell us that heaven is
simply the company of God, and hell the deprivation
of it.   And as God is the highest beauty, the highest
truth, and the highest good, it may be that hell is
nothing but that state in which souls only look after
themselves, their backs turned to the great struggles
of the Universal Mind, while heaven may be that
other plane where we can set our hands to the
service of the God of Battles for good—the idea of
Mr. Bernard Shaw in " Man and Superman," coin-
ciding strangely in this respect with the theology of
orthodox trinitarians, who acknowledge a god of
strife, a god who dies and rises again, together with
the immovable motor of the First Person and the
spermatic Logos of the Holy Ghost.

A theory like this may convince the reason that it
is useless to aim at the conquest of happiness.   Do
what we may we shall not be happy, nor shall we
make others happy.   I am not a Socialist because
I believe the working classes will be happy under
Socialism ; I am a Socialist because I believe that
Socialism is just and because I hope that Socialism
will relieve their minds from the economic burden
and free them for the exertion of higher activities.
Thus, in the individual, the legitimate desire to
solve the problem of love and health and bread does
not mean that happiness is achieved in the solution,
but that the solution gives the capacity for facing

other and higher problems.   On the other hand,
the ideal of ambition is illicit ; for the power that
the ambitious man desires—money, success, or domination—is purely relative to other men, and he can
only solve his own problem by creating it for others.
In this matter of power, therefore, it is not enough
for us to persuade ourselves that power does not
bring happiness with it ; it is likewise indispensable
that the law shall lay down for us limits beyond
which we cannot trespass.   Hence the necessity for
reviving an organization such as, for instance, the
old Guilds, in which the ambitions of the individuals
can have free play only within certain prescribed
limits.

The reason why I never developed this theory of
the automatism of pleasure and pain is that reflection persuaded me that it is not the reason which
must be convinced of the inevitable futility of the
idea of happiness.   The idea of happiness has never
taken up much space in the world of reason.   In
the history of philosophy it is an idea very much
of a secondary order.   Only the Stoics and the
Epicureans made happiness the central conception
of their doctrine, and the Stoics and Epicureans
were, at their best, third-class philosophers.   The
faculty of our souls in which happiness occupies
the greatest space is not the reason, but the imagination.   It is an ideal of the imagination, not of the
reason.   It will therefore be prudent for us to allow
the novelists, and not the thinkers, to show the
respectable public the foolishness of happiness.

And this is the great function of the novel.   What
is a novel ?   The description of an aspect of the
human soul personified in an imaginary figure, which
is made to live and die, to suffer and rejoice, within
the framework of society and nature.   Society and
ture are insensible to the happiness and unhap-

piness, to the life and death, of the protagonist of
the novel. It is all the same whether the novel deals
with Don Quixote de la Mancha, the altruist, or with
Sir Willoughby Patterne, the egoist. Every hero
of a novel is like a ship which, on leaving port,
bears in her hull the torpedo which is going to
sink her. But there is a difference between Don
Quixote and Sir Willoughby. When Don Quixote
dies, Quixotism remains in the air, a cultural value
that we have to serve ; when Sir Willoughby leaves
the scene his egoism carries with it a portion of our
own. In both cases the imaginative ideal of happiness within us has received a shock. We have learnt
to rejoice and to suffer with the joys and sufferings
of the hero of the work without suffering or enjoying
wholly, but as if the succession of joys and sufferings
were inevitable. And, as the hero of the novel is
but a part of ourselves, we have also learnt a little
to see our own joys and sufferings fading away
before our eyes, as if they were the joys and sufferings of another person. We have learnt, that is to
say, to rise a little above ourselves. And this is
the " catharsis " of the novel.

THE IDEAL OF LUXURY

A VISITOR to England has remarked that English women, amid the stress of war, have effected a complete revolution in fashion. The traveller meant by his observation that neither had the Germans been able to frighten Englishmen nor had Englishmen begun to realize the importance of the war, since after nine months of the most sanguinary campaign in history, frivolous women went on being as frivolous as before.

Nevertheless, the feminine frivolity which it reveals is not the most important feature of ' this observation. What is important is that this revolution of fashions points to the fact that in the large cities there are hundreds of thousands of people engaged, in time of war, in spinning, weaving, cutting out, designing, trimming, and distributing clothing for women who still have their wardrobes crammed with garments. Many of these elegant women are not frivolous. Some of them are working hard at organizing and conducting hospitals and attending to poor refugees. Did they fully realize what they were doing when they got unnecessary clothing made for themselves by people whose time would at that moment be more profitably occupied, for instance, in making uniforms for soldiers?

The war has taught one periodical, which is certainly not a revolutionary organ, the *Statist*, that " the real wealth of the world consists of the skill of the inhabitants of the world." " It is the labour, the industry, the skill, the intelligence, and the experience of the men which really make the wealth, and therefore is the wealth." This "journal of practical finance and trade" has learnt this lesson because it has seen that "the supply of labour in the great factories that turn out munitions of war is not able to cope with the emergency. . . . It is the want of men that is really felt." "An abundance of what is called wealth is of practically no use without the men to turn it into the forms in which it is specially useful." "Our Navy has control of the seas ; our imports and exports are practically up to the normal ; we can obtain food, raw materials, and everything we want in any quantities we please ; and yet, while all materials are in plenty, the chiefs of the Army are calling out that the operations of the war are being protracted simply because of the want of abundant supplies of munitions."

Every reader of these words will rejoice to think that even City papers have begun to understand that true economics is that which interprets figures of production and consumption, or imports and exports, in human terms, and not human activities in figures of employers' profits. The statement is true: Real wealth lies in the capacity to direct human activities into the moulds in which they are especially useful. Only, this capacity is obstructed by capitalism. It is, perhaps, necessary for England, in time of war, that all women who work in factories should be making uniforms or bandages, or tending the wounded, or cultivating the gardens of England. But capitalism says that these things must not be ; insists that these women shall devote their energies to making unnecessary garments ; decrees that their activity shall be dissipated in the production of luxuries ; and, in obedience to the will of capitalism, the labour of hundreds of thousands of women is still wasted in producing luxuries.

The worst of capitalism is that it grants to private individuals the right to spend as they like accumulated capital. A nobleman in the Middle Ages was as much bound to his land as his own serfs. He could not sell it ; he could not spoil it, or give over arable land to pasturage and hunting. He was a functionary. But a modern rich man may spend in a few years, if it please him, the capital accumulated by three hard-working generations ; and it is even possible for him to demoralize a fourth generation in the process of spending his money on luxuries and vices. But if this personal liberty is bad, the existence of capital is good. The savings of one generation are the tools of the next. Although capital may be in incompetent hands, its existence is preferable to its non-existence, because it is always possible for a Chancellor of the Exchequer to make it pass into better hands. The existence of capital enabled England to buy from other countries the munitions and food she needed for her great war. That shows us that Ruskin exaggerated when he said, " There is no wealth but life." This is one of those paradoxes which ought to be destroyed by the truism of " Wealth is wealth and life is life." Wealth is not life. Wealth is power, and power is an instrument for life, but not life. In the same way as in the individualistic societies of the past, socialistic societies of the future will have to devote part of their efforts to accumulating wealth for coming generations. Thrift will be a virtue in socialistic societies as it is now. The only truth in Ruskin's paradox is that wealth ought not to be accumulated at the expense of life, for human life is a higher value than wealth. Between thrift

and life there is a permanent conflict which only
wisdom can go on solving. But this does not mean
that there is harmony between life and luxury.
Luxury is precisely the destruction of wealth
without profiting life. Luxury is, then, an evil.
And not only so in this society, but in every
conceivable society.

Well, then, the thesis of this chapter is that the
production of articles of luxury is a waste of human
energy which should not be tolerated in a well-
regulated society. From this thesis it is to be
deduced that no man or woman (apart, of course,
from invalids, old people, and children) should have
the right to consume any material objects other
than those strictly necessary for their health and
for the efficacy of the social function they fulfil.
But modern economists answer these old attacks
on waste by saying that the conception of luxury
is relative, and one that cannot be determined
objectively, for, they say: " It is not a luxury at
all if a rich man drinks a glass of wine at his
meals, while this consumption would mean a luxury
on the table of a poor man." Are they right?

As has been indicated, everything is an article
of luxury that does not benefit the health or the
efficiency of producers. With this definition it is
admitted that those economists are right who speak
of the relativity of luxury. The books in my study
are not a luxury for me, for I use them in my
production. But in the study of a rich man who
did not read them, such books would be an unnecessary luxury. A Stradivarius is not a luxury
in the hands of Ysaye ; but the ten or twelve
Stradivariuses which hung idly on the walls of the
late Mr. Morgan's room were certainly luxuries.
That luxury is relative does not mean that it is
indefinable. The operation of defining is carried

out precisely by means of relations. From a subjective point of view, whatever is unnecessary for
a producer is a luxury, however necessary, it may
be for somebody else.

But here, it would seem, a difficulty begins.
Some years ago a woman said to me: "What
are luxuries for others are necessities for me." I
understood the hint, and had the saving strength
of will to turn my back on her. A "young exquisite
from the Pall Mall shop-windows," to use a phrase
of Oscar Wilde's, told me that he could not dress
on less than five hundred pounds a year. Perhaps
he was right; but a well-regulated society would
ask every man and woman: "Do you produce
more than you consume? All honour to you! Do
you consume more than you produce? Then you
are a thief." In nine cases out of ten the persons
who demand luxuries are themselves luxuries, and
as such unnecessary. In a well-regulated society
there would be no place for them.

But there are cases in which luxuries are considered necessary for persons fulfilling necessary
functions. The papers published an address delivered by the Dean of Canterbury in which he
said that, after trying hard very often to abstain
completely from alcoholic drinks, on the humble
ground of war economy, he found that the consumption of some little quantity of alcohol was
necessary for his work. Richard Wagner, too, in
his letters to Frau Wille, said that luxury was necessary for the full development of his personality.
But we do not know to which personality he referred.
Wagner was, at one and the same time, both a
musician of genius and a charlatan who wanted
to be talked about. As a musician, Wagner produced almost all his work before 1871, the year
in which he ceased to live as a poor man; and

if he had gone on being poor it is probable that in the last twelve years of his life he would not have produced less, but more. It is not by any means certain, then, that Wagner the musician needed luxury at all. As a charlatan, Herr Wagner has no interest for us. If he shows us that luxury is necessary for his music, we shall not haggle over giving him what he asks for. Once the need of it is proved to us, nobody will wish to deprive the Dean of Canterbury of his beer.

To this argument it only remains to be added that the personal necessity of luxury is not a sufficient reason for its preservation. Subjective necessities may be of very strange kinds. Jack the Ripper may tell us with entire sincerity that he found it necessary to murder a woman every two months. Luxuries must have been authorized socially before individuals can give themselves to them.

So far we have only denied the subjective necessity of luxury and the right of the individual to it. We must now discuss its objective value. You know the argument which is most commonly brought forward in defence of luxury. It may be summed up in these words: that the production of luxuries enables the poor to live. In support of this vulgar argument Mommsen has, in his "History of Rome," coined a phrase already classical: "The luxury of the great cities enriches many industrial hands, and nourishes more poor people than the alms given from the love of one's neighbour." The opinion of Mommsen, however, may not be that of the economists. Against his phrase can be set this remark of Professor Marshall ("Economics of Industry," p. 412): "Perhaps £100,000,000 annually are spent even by the working classes, and £400,000,000 by the rest of the population of England, in ways that do little or nothing towards making life nobler or truly happier."

Mommsen might reply to Professor Marshall that his statement held good. And so, indeed, it does. Once Rome allowed her Senators to make themselves masters of Italian soil, expropriate the labourers, and drive them to the metropolis after having taken away their land, the Roman people had no choice but to starve or to set about serving the caprices of the wealthy—sadly regretting, with Horace, those good old times when the private rents of Rome were small, but the common great: —

> Privatus illis census erat brevis
> Commune magnus.—(Carm. II, 15.)

To deny that the luxury of the rich enables the poor to live would be to deny the evidence of our senses. The luxury of the rich enables the poor to live, certainly ; but it likewise withdraws him from every useful social function. The article of luxury is sterile. If a man spends a hundred pounds on a ring, the hundred pounds will help the jeweller and his workmen to live ; but the jewel itself will not serve to produce new wealth. If the hundred pounds were spent on machinery, the money would enable the manufacturer and his workmen to live, but the machinery itself would serve to produce fresh wealth. The money which enters Monaco is divided, to a great extant, among the poor inhabitants of the principality. But when did the great hotels of Nice fulfil the more useful social function ?—when they served only, to satisfy the caprices of the idle rich, or—this year—when they were utilized by the French Republic as hospitals for those who fell sick or were wounded in the war? And ought not what happens in time of war to happen also in time of peace? Would it not be better if the mild climate of the Riviera were enjoyed by manual labourers or intellectuals fatigued by their daily toil rather than by idle rich who do not need rest, but work?

The luxury of the rich enables the poor to live, true. But what society requires is not merely that the poor shall live, but that they shall fulfil functions useful to society. The licentiousness of the rich man enriches the prostitute. But what society needs is not that the prostitute shall be enriched, but that there shall be no prostitutes. Avarice is usually condemned because it withdraws from society a capital which society requires. The censure is justified. Money, like blood, is life when it runs, but death when it stops. But the spendthrift is no less a culprit than the miser ; for the spendthrift withdraws from society activities which society requires as much at least as capital. Perhaps the greatest crime of the miser is that his accumulations of wealth make the spendthrift possible after him. For if it is an evil that the miser should withdraw, and therefore poison, blood from circulation, it is worse still that the spendthrift should infect with it all the rest. For how much has society not lost by the conversion of twenty workmen into twenty caddies?

Economists are usually unfriendly to laws against luxury, for, as they say, " the regulation of consumption is much less attainable than the regulation of production." And this chapter has not been written to urge the resurrection of laws such as those of the thirteenth century which prohibited the German nobility from wearing shoes with a point more than two feet long, the middle classes shoes with a point of more than one foot, and the other classes with more than six inches. But the greater problem of luxury is not that of consumption, but that of production. The iniquity of luxury, does not consist in the fact that the individual uses up his income in a bad way, but ,precisely in the fact that luxury creates an industry, which withdraws a large number of people from useful work.

Several Americans had prophesied that within a few years England would cease to be an industrial nation and become the playground for the entire Anglo-Saxon world, her fields given up to golf, to deer-hunting, to pheasant-shooting, to fox-hunting, and to the production of rare flowers and race-horses ; her poor men and women devoted to serving the rich as tailors and modistes, music-hall players, palmists, novelists, sellers of drinks and papers, etc. These prophecies have not been realized, and England still possesses 'a number of people accustomed to serious work ; she has been able to organize an army in her hour of stress, and to make uniforms, guns, ammunition, and ships ; and it is still possible that we may see the great stores of Harrods' and Selfridge's, and the shops in Bond Street, turned into shirt-factories for the soldiers, exactly as the Nice hotels have been turned into military hospitals.

We now see that the *Statist*—the " journal of practical finance and trade "—has rightly observed with the occasion of the war that the true wealth of England consists not in capital, but in " the labour, the industry, the skill, the intelligence, and the experience of men." Capital accumulated in private hands has done nothing but soften and enervate men and women, withdrawing them from really useful functions and turning them into servants of the rich and their whims. The *Statist*,

to be quite logical, should now undertake the propaganda of some social system, such as that of the
Guilds, which would not permit ' individuals to
accumulate capital whose possession enables them
to exploit or demoralize other people. In this way
it would take advantage, for times of peace, of
the great lesson which the 'war has taught it.

ART AND LUXURY

MANY artists feel anxious when they think of the possible reaction the war may have on the life of the arts and on culture in general. As war implies destruction of wealth in large proportions, these people have the impression that for many years to come men will devote their activities exclusively to re-making their lost fortunes in an existence of poverty and toil in which there will be neither time for leisure nor money for luxuries. Believing that the function of art is sumptuary or decorative, they conclude that if, in the next few years, there will be no money for luxuries, there will be none for the arts either ; and they fear that, in the absence of Mæcenases, the rose-bush of the arts will wither throughout the lands of Europe, as the flora and fauna of the high steppes of Asia died out when Divine Providence removed to other regions of the globe the clouds that fertilized them with their rain.

This belief that art is one of the articles of luxury is so widespread, not merely among the Philistines but among artists themselves, that if you ask a painter what is the object of a picture you will be told in most cases that " the object of a picture is to adorn a wall." The answer is commendable in its humility. By it the painter is placed in the category of artisans—carpet-weavers, furni-ture-makers, or paper-hangers ; and even when placed in this category the painter is not the first among the artisans, but the last. For, in truth, the most decorative picture ever painted will always be less decorative than a mirror, a panoply of arms, a velvet curtain, or a chandelier, since 'the material a painter makes use of, his poor colours, will always be less luxurious and less rich than marble and metal and light and velvet.

The curious thing is that this absurd idea that art is an article of luxury has been spread by the same men who gave up their lives to waving the banner of art for art's sake. I say it is a curious thing because the decorative conception of art is expressed by the formula of art for luxury's sake, and this formula is obviously incompatible with that of art for art's sake, unless we are prepared to agree to the proposition that art and luxury are one and the same thing. Shall we agree to this, just for the moment? Anatole France prophesied ironically in one of his books that there would come a day when the famous actresses of Paris, instead of declaiming and singing on the stage, would present themselves at the footlights, completely naked, and each of them carrying a bar of gold ; and the public would applaud with the maximum of enthusiasm the naked woman who exhibited the biggest bar of gold. I do not suppose any other arguments are needed to show that luxury is not art. But the fact that the standard-bearers of art for art's sake—Théophile Gautier in France and Oscar Wilde in England—were also the propagandists of art for luxury's sake makes it clear that there was a fundamental error in their attitude, an error that rendered it unstable ; and if we can root out this error 'we shall have killed two birds with one stone: art for art's sake and art for luxury's sake.

What is most surprising in the formula of art

for art's sake is that it refers to a novelty which contradicts the artistic traditions of a thousand years. Beethoven did not write the Heroic Symphony solely for the joy of making music, but he wrote it in the service of the French Revolution and in honour of its hero, General Bonaparte. Milton did not write " Paradise Lost " with the sole aim of bequeathing a poem to us, but in order that—

> I may assert eternal Providence,
> And justify the ways of God to men.

And Michelangelo did not paint the Sistine Chapel only for the purpose of decorating a wall, but to depict before our eyes the omnipotent will of Jehovah. You may tell me that I have chosen examples of our own Christian art. But the Greeks, the most artistic people that ever lived . . . " The Greeks had no art-critics," wrote Wilde in his " Intentions." But the truth about Greek art is much deeper than that. The truth is that the Greeks never spoke of beauty as something distinct from knowledge or morality, religion or life. The word " beautiful " was never used by them to designate an autonomous cultural value. The ideal of every good Hellene was to be a perfect gentleman, and a gentleman could not achieve perfection if he did not die a noble death. Both of the perfect gentleman and of a noble death the Greeks said they were beautiful. And the most artistic people the world has known never used the word " beautiful " without giving to it the moral signification of perfection.

The Greeks had no art-critics because they had no æsthetics ; but æsthetics is philosophy and not art. The depuration of the conception of beauty, the distinction between the form and matter of the

11

work of art, is necessary for the philosopher, and perhaps also for the art-critic. But for the artist it is unnecessary. Not only unnecessary: it is impossible to achieve. In the heat of artistic creation the form is not and cannot be more than love for the matter of the work. No artist has ever conceived a work from pure love of art, but from love of a given subject. Art is love, and love does not love itself. Not even Gautier and Wilde could practise the doctrine of art for art's sake. Their formula can be accepted only as a battle-cry guiding art towards its emancipation from the tyranny of didactics. It was a device of some value against the people who sought to turn art into a weapon of pedestrian puritanism. But when Gautier and Wilde tried to separate art from morality and knowledge they found that art for art's sake was a wheel of wind wheeling the wind ; and to find sustenance for it they had to harness it to the service of luxury, vice, and decoration.

Far from being a pure artist, Gautier was the apostle of a moral idea. A contemporary of the Sardanapalian pictures of Delacroix, of the " Orientales " of Victor Hugo, of the Orientalist ethics of the Saint-Simonists, and of the first French expedition to Northern Africa, Théophile Gautier preaches the redemption of the world by means of a universal animalism. People are now in the habit of regarding his novels, " Fortunio " and " Mademoiselle de Maupin," as pornographic books ; but they are more than that. They are exhortations to pornography. Comte Georges, in " Fortunio," has a politico-social idea, the idea that the State should compel beautiful women to exhibit themselves naked from time to time so that taxpayers should not lose the sense of colour and form. For Gautier, of course, love and lust are the same thing: " No woman resists so obstinately as virtue with ill-shaped knees " ; " One woman is as good as another, if she is as pretty " ; " Among beautiful and strong natures love is gratitude for satisfaction."

But this animalism of Gautier's is in a way a derivation. Gautier was primarily a reader of the works of other writers. He read with so much impressionability that at the end of a single perusal he was able to repeat by heart 185 lines of Victor Hugo's verses. For his friends he was a kind of dictionary. He hated the reality of his age because " in this civilization, which cares only about raising soap and candle makers on pedestals, one loses the sensation of the beautiful." Thus the formula of art for art's sake had for Gautier no other meaning than that of a mediatization of reality, an escape from it. He could not look at a woman or a landscape without asking himself, " Who would have painted that? " He would call a garden " a Watteau park." He remarked of his Fortunio and his Musidora: " It was a Giorgione beside a Lawrence." Only when he realized that a man could not go on evoking works of art all his life did he get beyond the formula of art for art's sake and annex it to the service of life. But Gautier's idea of life, based, as he based it, on the negation of morality and knowledge, was that of an animalism scarcely disguised under the veil of luxury.

The case of Oscar Wilde is almost identical with that of Théophile Gautier, whom he often quotes in his writings. " The Picture of Dorian Gray " was not written merely for art's sake. Wilde tells us that he wished to express by Dorian Gray " the true realization of a type of mind which they have often dreamed in Eton or Oxford days, a type that was to combine something of the real culture of the scholar with all the grace and distinction and

perfect manner of a citizen of the world." Dorian
Gray is not merely a character in a novel, but the
incarnation of " a new Hedonism that was to re-
create life and to save it from that harsh, uncomely
puritanism that is having, in our own day, its curious
revival." The fact that Dorian Gray comes to an
unfortunate end in the novel—and in the life of
Oscar Wilde—does not mean that the author
repudiates his motto, " to cure the soul by means
of the senses, and the senses by means of the
soul," formulated again in the phrase, " culture and
corruption." Dorian Gray dies as the heroes of
tragic dramas and of novels of the first order had
to die—" Don Quixote," " Madame Bovary,"
" Wuthering Heights," or " Anna Karenina."
Such heroes die because one of the categories
of art is the religious ; and the religious category
is essentially Death and Resurrection. But Dorian
Gray is not killed by Wilde out of punishment, but
out of love, because he is a hero ; and Wilde
expects to see Hedonism arising from his grave,
as Christianity arose from the Cross. And there
are still people who see in Oscar Wilde the pre-
cursor and martyr of the new Hedonism : " culture
and corruption."

But that is not to preach art for art's sake,
but art for luxury's sake, for pleasure's sake, art
for the sake of " refinement " or decoration. And
not art alone, but life itself—life as understood by
the " smart set." The main chapter of " Dorian
Gray " is certainly not more than an idealization of
the " smart set." " Like Gautier," writes Wilde,
" Dorian Gray was one for whom ' the visible
world existed ' " ; " And, certainly, to him life itself
was the first, the greatest, of the arts " ; " His
modes of dressing had their marked influence on
the young exquisites of the Mayfair balls and Pall

Mall windows " ; " The Roman ritual had always a great attraction for him " ; " And for a season he inclined to the materialistic doctrines of the '.Darwinismus' movement in Germany " ; " Yet no theory of life seemed to him to be of any importance compared with life itself " ; " And so he would now study perfumes, and the secrets of their manufacture, distilling heavily scented oils, and burning odorous gums from the East " ; " At another time he devoted himself entirely to music, and in a long latticed room, with a vermilion-and-gold ceiling and walls of olive-green lacquer, he used to give curious concerts " ; " On one occasion he took up the study of jewels " ; " Then he turned his attention to embroideries." Here you have the complete circle: dandyism, religion, " Darwinismus," perfumes, embroideries, jewels, and music " in a long latticed room."

This description of Dorian Gray, of course, is nothing more than an idealized paraphrase of Théophile Gautier's " Notice " of Charles Baudelaire, prefixed to the definitive edition of " Les Fleurs du Mal," the book that Oscar Wilde's hero possessed, " bound in some Nile-green skin that has been powdered with gilded nenuphars and smoothed with hard ivory." As Baudelaire had really lived, Gautier could not tell us that he went to balls covered with 560 pearls, like Dorian Gray ; but he does tell us, giving all the details, that Baudelaire enjoyed symphonies and perfumes, insolent-looking coiffures, " in which something of the actress and the courtesan was mingled," cats which were attracted by essences, " cats that the smell of valerian threw into a kind of ecstatic epilepsy," cold, cunning, and perverse women, " who carry into the soul the vice of the body," and the Black Venus of Madagascar.

The coincidence between Gautier and Wilde is due to the fact that there was common to them a strange belief that both Nature and the human mind had exhausted their creative capacities. Life had already engendered its riches: it only remained to enjoy them. Art had already produced its wonders: they had only to be recorded. From this vision of Nature as something finished is born the animalism of Gautier, and from his conception of art comes his technique, which consists in reproducing the image that another artist had wrested from reality. In the case of Oscar Wilde, too, his parasitic Hedonism springs from his retrospective philosophy of life ; and from his retrospective æsthetic comes his conception of modern art as a mere evocation of ancient art. In his essay, "The Critic as Artist," he goes the length of declaring resolutely that " as civilization progresses and we become more highly organized, the elect spirit of each age, the critical and cultured spirits, will grow less and less interested in actual life, and *will seek to gain their impressions almost entirely from what art has touched*." Both in life and in art his ideal was marginal—luxury.

In this cult there was the mistaken but saving conviction that an article of luxury must be carefully elaborated by a skilful artificer. I say " saving " because it led Gautier and Wilde to perfect their manner of using the material they worked with—words—and to give to other artists the sound advice not to be satisfied, when executing a work of art, with their good moral intentions. But I say " mistaken " because in the article of luxury the essential thing is not the form but the rarity of the material—gold, skin, or diamonds—or the quantity of labour displayed at our command. The object of luxury resembles the object of art in that both are expressions of power ; but, while the object of luxury is only, the expression of property or monopoly, the work of art tells us, through the power of the means of expression, that man is the master of Nature. Craftsmanship means power. In the object of luxury, the thing to be shown is the power of the proprietor. In the work of art the essential thing is the power of the artist.

The world of Gautier and Wilde is dead. The coming generations, whether they like it or not, must be the children of this war that found Europe dancing the Argentine tango and will leave it dancing to the tune of St. Vitus. The horrors and the bloodshed show us that either Nature or the human mind has at any rate lost its powers of destruction. But even now, in the middle of night, one may perceive new streaks of hope and of creation. The very need of knowing the causes and conditions of this catastrophe must bring us nearer the elements of human nature, and hence into the possibilities of a better life. This may involve a whole renovation of politics, ethics, economics, and of all the humanities. We have to think in the next few years for the half-century, during which we ceased to think. And with the new ideals will come the desire to realize them immediately.

In this desire immediately to realize ideals we must see one of the categories of artistic creation as distinct from mere evocation. The secret of art will not be unravelled until we have a philosophy capable of constructing a satisfactory æsthetic. All the æsthetics conceived hitherto have told the truth ; not one of them saw more than partial aspects of the beautiful. The beautiful is more than a synthesis between what is and what ought to be (Kant), more than the perceptible apparition of the idea (Hegel), more than pure feeling (Cohen), more than the intuition of the individual (Croce), and much, much more than an article of luxury. Humboldt said that a work of art placed human nature "at a point whence rays surged out in all directions into the infinite." It is a union of reality and ideal, of present and eternity, of soul and body, of the empiric and the necessary ; a present realization of religious hopes ; a reconciliation of man with all the spiritual and material elements, external and internal, past and future, of his life ; because it is a sign—but only a sign, not a proof: not even a sincere promise—that this world has a meaning.

That is why art will not cease because Europe may become poorer. The poorer we are the more we shall need it, for it will not be possible for us to lull our souls with the narcotic of luxury. Lyric poetry was never paid for in England, except in the case of Lord Tennyson. No other Mæcenases have fed it but the tears of the poets. And lyrics are one of the things that make of England one of the faces of God upon the earth.

HEDONIST OBJECTIONS

ONCE upon a time there was a caliph of Bagdad who was so much overcome by a black melancholy that neither the houris of his harem, nor the victories of his troops, nor the reading of the Koran could cheer him up. "You will be cured," said a soothsayer to him, "when you put on the shirt of a happy man." The caliph sent his viziers out all over the world in search of a happy man's shirt. But they found only one happy man. He was a fisherman, and he had no shirt. If they had remembered this story, the men who drew up the Constitution of the United States would not have included happiness among the objects whose pursuit they proposed to their people. It is not an aim which we can set up for ourselves. Its region is that of dreams, not that of will. It is an ideal of the imagination, not of the reason. For that I exclude it from the results which we have a right to expect from a good social régime. Reason permits us to believe that we shall succeed in creating an economic system in which every man may be contented with his work, since he ought to believe it to be just. But work will always be painful. "In the sweat of thy face shalt thou eat bread" (Gen. iv. 9). Even in idleness we shall not be happy—nor in the grave— nor in paradise.

The real cause of the failure of democracy is that it cares much more for happiness than for justice. And democracy will continue to fail until it is cured of its hedonism or ideal of pleasure. Not that a perfect cure is possible, for hedonism —its real name is lust—is one of the aspects of original sin, and, therefore, ineradicable in human nature. What can be done—what has been done for the last four thousand years, and what it will be necessary to do for the next ten thousand— is to refute its arguments, and, by continually refuting them, keep up a state of eternal vigilance against it.

There is no doubt that the most lamentable con- sequence of capitalistic industrialism is what may be called the de-spiritualization of labour. The introduction of mechanical tools into factories led to the mechanization of the soul of the workmen and snatched from them what some economists regard as the supreme "happiness"—the love of work for the sake of the work itself. A craftsman of the Middle Ages might well feel a certain amount of affection for the chair he made, for he produced it in its entirety from the felling of the tree in the wood to the nailing on of the leather seat in his own workshop. But in a modern factory a certain number of the workmen have nothing to do with the finished chairs—the fireman who throws the coal into the furnace, the engineer who looks after the machinery, the lad who oils the engines. Each chair has ceased to be an individual production differing in quality from its fellows ; it is, instead, turned out to a standard pattern and flung on the market.

How is this problem to be solved? As the way in which it is presented to the eyes of a spectator is mainly æsthetic—the ugliness of mechanically produced things—the primary solution which occurs to him is likewise æsthetic. Such was the solution recommended by Ruskin and William Morris, if I interpret their spirit correctly : " Let us make an end of this mechanical capitalistic production. Let us restore the beautiful little industries of the mediæval villages. Let us turn society into a corporation of artists who shall humbly submit to the law of love and discover their joy in the production of beautiful things until the whole world shall become a temple of beauty." And it would, of course, be absurd to try to argue with this dream, in favour or against it. It was a beautiful dream ; far be it from me to try to destroy it.

When we leave the world of dreams and enter the world of reality, we find ourselves faced with the fact that the production of beautiful things does not make their producers happy. Lace is beautiful. It is quite possible that a wealthy lady may be happy in making lace to adorn the mantle of the Virgin who, she believes, has saved her son's life. But the occupation of the lace-makers of Alençon is one of the most monotonous and worst paid on the face of the earth. Gold is beautiful. But the powder of the quartz turns into stone the lungs of the men who extract it from the Rand mines. Pearls are beautiful. But the men who gather them in Ceylon have to dive with a forty-pound weight round their neck in waters frequented by sharks. A good Havana cigar is beautiful. But it owes its perfume to the fact that it is prepared in a workshop the windows of which are never opened, and in which the red dust of the tobacco makes the workman who rolls it cough incessantly. Gobelin tapestries are beautiful ; but the men and women who weave them work on the wrong side of the design. Beautiful things, articles of luxury, are made in precisely the same way as useful things, for the sake of earning one's bread. If the Alençon lace-makers had the choice of making lace or mending their children's stockings, they would choose the stockings. And the production of luxuries is even more painful than the production of necessities. For, after all, necessities are necessary. Their production is a slavery imposed upon us by Nature. But the production of luxuries is unnecessary; it is a slavery imposed upon us, not by Nature, but by the wealth of a few men. To obey Nature is not degrading. But it is degrading to be compelled to undertake unnecessary work for the satisfaction of a whim.

These examples show that you cannot make workmen happy merely by utilizing their energies in the production of beautiful things. And although their unhappiness has been aggravated by capitalism, it would not disappear with it; for repugnance to work, whatever it may be, lies above and beyond any economic system. Epictetus has already remarked: "Every art is wearisome, in the learning of it, to the untaught and unskilled. Yet things that are made by the arts immediately declare their use, and for what they are made, and in most of them is something attractive and pleasing. And thus when a shoemaker is learning his trade it is no pleasure to stand by and observe him, but the shoe is useful, and moreover not unpleasing to behold. And the learning of a carpenter's trade is very grievous to an untaught person who happens to be present, but the work done declares the need of the art. But far more is this seen in music, for if you are by where one is learning it will appear the most painful of all instructions; but that which is produced by the musical art is sweet and delightful to hear, even to those who are untaught in it."

The ideal of having every article of use perfected into beauty reminds me of an old gentleman in a dusty Spanish town who was as fond of walking as of keeping untarnished the lustre of his boots. Too poor to pay for a shoeblack as often as he wished, every ten minutes he stopped his walking, took out of his pockets blacking, brushes, and rags, hid himself in a porch, and painfully restored in his shoes the gloss of shining jet. We used to look at him compassionately, but if a man had served him as shoeblack for ten hours a day the mood of our souls would have been anger and not compassion. I cannot forget the impression made upon me by my first sight of spotless Berlin : " In this city are there any other people than sweeps and window-cleaners ? " It looks as if the people who maintain this ideal want the Guilds to multiply the labours of humanity by adding to the work now wasted in the production of superfluities for the rich the exertions involved in the production of luxuries for everybody. But I hope that as soon as the workmen get the control of their economy they will say : " Enough of this foolery, and let us live plainly, that our hands may rest, and our minds may work, and if our hands prefer labour to leisure let them accomplish works of art, in the free spirit of Ariel, ' to answer thy best pleasure.' "

Socrates believed that philosophers, after death, met together on a pure earth and, freed from the blindness of the flesh, went on conversing among themselves and inquiring into the essence of things. That means that Socrates was content with his job. And there can be no more noble activity than that of observing men classifying the ideas which govern their conduct, and deducing thence the supreme idea of the Good. But of one thing I am sure.

The day on which a new truth occurred to Socrates, and on which, in ordering this thought in his mind —excited and absorbed in his work of verifying the fecundity of his discovery in every direction— the time passed without his realizing it—that day of intense pleasure had to be paid for, as all other thinkers have to pay for it, by nights of insomnia and days of lethargy. For the flame of inspiration, like the flame of love, does not give us its radiance for nothing, but, as it passes away, leaves part of our spirit turned into ashes.

Happiness has been defined as the free exercise of our faculties. "We are happy," it has been said, "when we are free, when our desires and doings run unimpeded on their way." I accept this definition as a good one in so far as it presents to us the subjective aspect of happiness. I myself prefer, of course, the objective definition, according to which happiness signifies favourable destiny, invariable fortune, or permanent pleasure. But if we analyse the subjective definition, we shall see that it denies that happiness is possible. For it is true enough that we should be happy if all "our desires and doings ran unimpeded on their way." But this is impossible ; for desires and doings do not run on the same road. When I was studying philosophy it occurred to me one day to run about the streets of a German town with a placard on my shoulders, saying : "I am the son of a hundred mothers." I did not do it, for not all our desires become doings. But what I meant to say by that phrase still seems to me to be true ; and it is this : We do not possess a single desire : we are the point where millions of desires cross and fight with one another. At every moment of our life we are seized with contrary desires. If we eat a cake we wish at the same

time to have it too ; if we ring the bells we
wish to be walking in the procession ; if we go
to a wedding we should like to be the bride, and
we should even like to be the dead man at a
funeral. Every act of will carries with it the
selection of a desire and the sacrifice of contrary
desires. And, if the realization of a desire is agreeable, the sacrifice of those which give way to the
victor is disagreeable. There never was and never
will be a man whose "desires and doings run
unimpeded on their way."

"Assuming," it is said, "that happiness is not
a mere figment of imagination . . ." Assuming
that, of course, I should be an eudemonist, but not
of the utilitarian sort, who want "the greatest
happiness of the greatest number," but of the kind
of Sir Willoughby Patterne, "the Egoist." Not
Guild Socialism would be my motto, but my own
selfish happiness. Perhaps good people think that
they cannot be happy so long as other people are
unhappy. This is at least a common thought among
social reformers. But not less common is the
indignation of unhappy social reformers against
other people because they feel happy under conditions of slavery in which they ought to feel unhappy.
People feel happy and unhappy under the most
disconcerting circumstances, unhappy in plenty and
happy in hunger. "Life is not so good nor so
bad as it is thought," wrote Maupassant at the end
of a novel. Ergo, happiness cannot be an objective
criterion of political or ethical conduct. Why should
responsibility—the responsibility in his labour that
we want for every workman—be an element of
happiness? Many will find happier the "I don't
care" attitude of the gipsy and the slave.
"Assuming happiness . . ." Yes, but the critical
philosophy was invented by Kant precisely that w

should not assume the validity, of dubious and superfluous hypotheses.

Well, then, if we cannot find happiness in the producers of beautiful things, shall we find it in their consumers? Let us call beautiful, if you will, those articles of luxury which are to be purchased in the expensive shops. Are the women happy who spend two or three thousand a year on dress? They are, perhaps, for five minutes, when they put on each new costume. They are even happier when other women envy them. And that is all. One writer has said that luxuries are stimulants, and he can say no more than that in their defence. No doubt they are stimulants ; but when we say that we say nothing. Crimes are stimulants for the activities of the police. The stimulation of articles of luxury is very easy to understand. They are unnecessary work which will stimulate people to work unnecessarily in order that they may consume unnecessary articles which will make other people work without any real necessity to justify their efforts. Does not this writer remember the legend of Ocnus and the Danaides? As fast as Ocnus wove his cord the she-ass by his side ate it ; and the Danaides are still in the infernal regions, vainly trying to fill with water the bottomless barrel. Ocnus and the Danaides were the men and women of the European hell until a year ago—and not under Divine sentence, but from a spontaneous love for the she-ass and the bottomless barrel, whose insatiable voracity they framed in Blue Books announcing the annual increase in the figures of production and consumption.

I entirely sympathize with the personal love of luxury. I feel it myself, too. If my dreams could fulfil themselves, I should be an Oriental despot, with a whole kingdom as my garden, twenty white elephants, three thousand slaves, and a harem. And I am not alone in these tastes. Every ascetic saint who lived on earth had in himself a natural man equally fond of a "natural defence of luxury." A saint is not more than a natural man in whom second thoughts have unnaturally developed a second artificial man, the moral or social one. That is why saints are so interesting. They have within themselves two different men in constant polemical dialogue. They are complex, fighting, restless. "To live in perfect calm," wrote Campoamor, the Spanish humorist, "either the soul or the body, is redundant." But natural men enjoy the serenity, of trees in a wood, and, though they, fight among themselves, just as the roots of trees contend for the sap of the land, they are serene inside—serene, monologist, and boring. So, when it is said, "There is nothing in the nature of man which says to him, 'Thou shalt not eat peaches in Brixton,'" I heartily assent.

The problem of luxury is not a problem of demand, but of supply. I want peaches in Bayswater, and many other things as well. The question is this other : Shall I get them? It is no use to reply, "It is only his pocket which talks." Of course, if I am rich, I can force starving people to satisfy my whims. Of course, of course. Through the might of money I could make the poor do almost everything. This is a fact, a legal fact. I could even buy a lawyer to defend it. But if we are Socialists we cannot believe it is right that the poor should exert themselves in ministering to our personal caprices when their labour is necessary to society elsewhere. When we theorize on things as they ought to be, and not as they are, we must postulate a State in which the power to command belongs to society and not to the rich. As we could no longer force other people to become directly or indirectly our servants, we should be bound to convince them by objective reasons of the social utility of their exertions in our personal service. Let me try, then, the reasons more frequently adduced by the upholders of luxury. If I fail with them I shall be obliged to sacrifice my luxuries, at least in our ideal republic.

The first, and weightiest, consists in minimizing the whole question. I can say, " The late Mr. Morgan with his ten Stradivariuses is a subject for ridicule, not for moralizing." It is a good argument. I should say to the workmen of a free republic : " Comrades, you can laugh at me as if I were a low comedian, but, please, give me £500 a week, as you gave in former times to low comedians." Well, the workmen would say : " We don't mind your £500. But, you know, Professor Marshall says that £500,000,000 are annually spent by the population of England in luxuries ' that do little or nothing towards making life nobler or truly happier.' This is a lot of money. It is 25 per cent. of the English national income. It is said that there are in England ten million people underfed, under-clothed, and under-warmed. If we gave to every one of them one shilling more per day we could feed, clothe, and warm properly these ten millions with £180,000,000 annually ; with £120,000,000 we could house them comfortably ; and with the other £200,000,000 we could promote the talents of the people for science and for art, so as to try to make a Florence and an Athens of every village of the kingdom. And which would be better, that we employ our labour in producing the material and spiritual things which satisfy our needs or the articles of luxury which are not really required either by our souls or by our bodies? "

Rebuked in the attempt to minimize the question, I should have recourse to the second argument, and would say: "But one cannot categorize luxury; what is or what is not luxury for an individual no one but himself can possibly decide." The reason would not stand a long debate. Luxury is already categorized. No visitors are allowed in hospitals for soldiers to bring eatables to the patients. "But they are ill," it is replied. Yes, they are ill. But the soldiers in camps are not ill, yet their food is also regulated, and they look splendid. The nurses wear uniforms. Luxury in dresses is forbidden to them, and the pretty ones are not less pretty for their uniforms. Private servants find equally regulated their food and dress and hours of work and recreation. And it is not their regulation which is wrong. What is wrong is the fact that the servants cannot regulate as well the dress, the food, and the life and work of their mistresses. One of my critics does not like "high and hard chairs." I agree with an assent that this time is not merely personal. "High and hard chairs" are luxuries, as they do not fulfil the proper function of chairs which are not luxuries, that of giving rest to tired bodies. The fact of giving names to some chairs proves my case that some are functional and good and some luxurious and bad. And if the chairs that are high for others may be low for me that does not imply that the size of chairs cannot be regulated; it can be regulated, and the regulation ought to be made according to their use.

We have seen that it is possible to decide what is necessity and what is luxury for a producer. But is it expedient to have these things regulated by the Guilds? The question of expediency is often complex. "All things are lawful for me, but all things are not expedient," wrote St. Paul (1 Cor. x. 23).

Many people are opposed to the regulation of the consumption of luxuries. So am I. So said I previously that "the greater problem of luxury is not that of consumption, but that of production." Provided that the labour of the workmen is not wasted in the production of silks and feathers and jewels and cigars and millinery when it is needed for the production of wool and food and guns and shells, there would not be necessary a regulation of consumption, because we should obtain practically the same results, the suppression of luxuries through the regulation of production, which would certainly prove to be of an easier attainment. Of course, this supremacy of the social will in economical matters may be called tyranny by parasitical individuals. But we know already what liberalism means in economics : it means capitalism, arbitrary freedom for the rich and compulsory slavery for the poor.

And, finally, our pleasure in pure art is of a superior kind to that produced in us by the possession or the contemplation of articles of luxury, however decorative they may be. The essential difference between ornamental art and pure art lies in the fact that ornamental art is but a mere adaptation of a useful object to the senses ; it is the gilding of the pill—the mask which seeks to conceal one effort with another. But pure art arises in a feeling of distance between the reality and the ideal ; it is a metaphor which raises the world of our senses to the moral plane, or makes the moral world descend to the region of the senses. Pure art is thus an anticipation of the ideal. It reveals to us the meaning of meaningless things. It tells us that there is a God behind the insensible crust of Nature. Its mission is religious and necessary. But, unfortunately, it is transient. It reveals the sense of things to the ephemeral intuition, but in the twinkling of a lightning flash.   It was only in a moment of enthusiasm that the poet could say :—

A thing of beauty is a joy for ever.

The more profound note is in the sonnet :—

Bright star, would I were steadfast as thou art.

The tragedy of beauty is that it has no yesterday nor to-morrow, and man lives only for a few minutes in the present.   Life is woven between perspectives and retrospects.   In it there are moments of pure beauty.   But I would not condemn my worst enemy to spend ten hours of every day of his life in reading the poetry that pleased him best.   In life there are also moments which appear to us to be happy. Happiness happens.   Just so, and nothing more.

At bottom I do not object to people who try to give an imaginative character to their ideal of Guild Socialism.   I, too, believe that when human labour is better organized there will remain an overflow of energy which the Guilds will spend in building cathedrals and palaces and laying out gardens.   The more universal the work is, and the more perfect the machinery employed in the production of necessary articles, the more surplus energy there will be.   But the foundation of the Guild idea must be ethical. We want Guilds because we cannot discover any other method of enabling labour to cease from being a commodity in the hands of the rich, or to secure for workmen a share in the control of and responsibility for their work.   We owe them this in justice. And in a court of justice people do not speak of beauty or of happiness.   I am not sure that the majority of men would prefer responsibility to passive obedience.   This is perhaps the tragedy of the *New Age*.   It is very possible that most of them would prefer obedience to responsibility. Suppose this is so : what should we do? Let men go on being content with their prosperous slavery, or try to awaken in every one of them the spirit of responsibility? In the face of this dilemma we cannot set up happiness as a criterion. It is the moral spirit that fires our propaganda.

But I have been dealing with a grave subject, and I must seek the help of weightier words than mine. Listen to Kant : " Happiness is everybody's solution. But it is not to be found anywhere in Nature, which is not susceptible of happiness or contentedness with circumstances. The only thing man can achieve is to deserve happiness." Are we downhearted? But when the moments of happiness and beauty are past there remain always the need of earning one's bread, the duty of being good and of inquiring what kind of thing is life, and the religious hope of not living in vain.

THE END OF ROMANTICISM

An objective conception of social life is gradually
becoming clearer in the minds of men. This conception tells us that men do not associate immediately with one another, but that every human
society—the family, the State, the workshop, the
farm—is an association of men and things—the
home, the native land, business, amusement, etc.
The laws are rules which arise directly from the
intermingling of men and things in society. As
this intermingling is made necessary by the interdependence of men, and is therefore original, the
law is also original and necessary. As men are
intertwined in many things, there are also many
laws for regulating the conduct of men with respect
to these things. Some laws relate to necessary or
economic things, others to good or moral things.
Societies are in a state of progress when the number
of good things is increased and their quality im-
proved ; they are stationary or in retrogression
when they cease to add to the number of their good
things or no longer preserve them. The social value
of every man depends upon his conduct with respect
to the things which are necessary or good for
society. His dignity depends upon his work.
Objective ethics teaches us that. We wish to found
a society in which rights shall be based on work
only. Objective politics tells us that.

This spells the end of Romanticism. Mr. T. E.
Hulme, in his Introduction to Sorel's " Reflections

upon Violence " (Allen and Unwin), has named romantics all those thinkers who do not believe in the fall of Adam. We shall apply the name of romantic to every one who believes that all men or some men are good in themselves, and that this goodness will be revealed as soon as the veils which hide it are torn away. Let us open, for example, Emerson's " Essays," and it, under the heading " Self-Reliance," we find a phrase like this, " Speak your latent conviction and it shall be the universal sense ; for the inmost in due time becomes the utmost," we shall say to ourselves, " There goes the romantic." And, after turning the sentence over in our minds, we shall add : " Flatterer ! The power of romanticism lies in flattery. It wants to make us believe that we are in reality much greater than we believe ourselves to be, and greater than others think us. But I know very well that the little I can find within myself is due to what men and things have taught me, and I know also that without that I should find nothing."

It is characteristic of the romantic to forget that things do exist. Emerson writes in another place : " An institution is the lengthened shadow of one man." " A man Cæsar is born, and for ages after we have a Roman Empire. Christ is born, and millions of minds so grow and cleave to His genius that He is confounded with virtue and the possible of man." Emerson, clearly enough, is speaking of the " Jesus of History " and not of the " Christ of Faith " when he tells us that Christianity took its rise in the " genius " of Jesus. And I do not know whether our objective conception of social life can be applied to theological problems. There is something in man which cannot be bound by laws. Remember the saying of Maeterlinck, another romantic : " Men, like mountains, are united only by their lowest parts ; their peaks rise solitary to the infinite." Perhaps it is the purpose of religions to unite mysteriously those peaks of the soul on which men try to escape from one another. But if our objective conception of life could embrace religious problems, we should say, against Emerson, that an institution is not the shadow of a man but a society of men around a thing, and that the Jesus of History could not create the Christ of Faith, but that the Jesus of History had to arise out of the Christ of Faith.

Carlyle, another romantic, would protest against this assertion : " For, as I take it, Universal History, the history of what man has accomplished in this world, is at bottom the history of the Great Men who have worked here." But let us reverse Carlyle's thesis, and say : " The history of Great Men is the history of what man has accomplished in this world." And where Carlyle tells us : " We cannot look, however imperfectly, upon a great man, without gaining something by him," let us read : " We cannot look, however imperfectly, upon a great *thing*, without gaining something by *it*." To Carlyle things are nothing but the clothes of his " Sartor Resartus." Underneath them his eyes discover the mind of man. " There is but one temple in the universe," he says with Novalis, that romantic of romantics, " and that is the Body of Man." And he adds on his own account : " *We* are the miracle of miracles—the great inscrutable mystery of God." Good ! This " inscrutable " mystery stands revealed in the pages of Carlyle's work " On Heroes." The " Great Mystery " is there to be seen. " The Great Man " is a mystery. Instead of analysing the Great Thing, Carlyle goes direct to the mystery. He does not speak to us of Shakespeare's dramas but of Shakespeare the man. By the same method the un-

scrupulous charlatanism of Frank Harris deduces
" Hamlet " from the love affairs of Shakespeare and
Mary Fitton.   But these men who explain great
works to us by great men, can they tell why it is that
great men are not great in all their works?   Why
Napoleon was great at Austerlitz and not at Water-
loo?   Why Cervantes is great in " Don Quixote "
and not in " Pérsiles y Segismunda "? Does it never
occur to them to suspect that the greatness which
they attribute to some men is theirs solely in consequence of the greatness of the things they have
made?

But the " Hero " of Carlyle and the " Representative Man " of Emerson maintain always a certain
nexus with things.   " Shakespeare's powerful merit,"
says Emerson, " may be conveyed in saying that
he, of all men, best understands the English language, and can say what he will."   " Each man
is by secret liking connected with some district of
Nature, whose agent and interpreter he is ;   as
Linnæus, of plants ; Hubert, of bees ;   Fries, of
lichens ; Von Mons, of pears ;   Danton, of atomic
forms ;   Euclid, of lines ;   Newton, of fluxions."
One sentence of Emerson even formulates the ideal
of an objective morality :   " It is for man to tame
the chaos."   Had Emerson insisted upon this
thought the American people would to-day be much
less pompous.   But two lines earlier he writes :
" Great men exist that there may be still greater
men," and a few pages before :   " Man can paint,
or make, or think, nothing but man "—an assertion
as false as characteristic of romanticism.

The " Hero " and the " Representative Man " are
still functionaries.   They serve as an example to the
many.   But Renan has said that the aim of the world
is to produce gods for whose maintenance the many
must work ;   these " gods " need not fulfil any func-

tion ; they will receive their food for nothing; at
the utmost, they will contemplate the labours and
the superstitions of the crowd.   And so, too, the
" Superman " of Nietzsche : " Now that all the gods
are dead we will that Superman live."   This Superman will serve only as an ornament : " I would be
the sun, for when he spreads his last rays over the
sea, even the humblest fishermen row with oars of
gold."   In this beautiful image we are not chiefly
moved by the gilding of the fishermen's oars, for
any day we may see them gilded by one of the new
producers who try to make of the theatre a gorgeous
banquet for the eyes.   But we are flattered as we
feel our beloved ego expand until it reaches the
farthest sun.   My expanded ego, my own ego, my
unique ego, multiplied by power ! My ego the
unique ! " The unique and its own," said Max
Stirner, the true forerunner of Nietzsche, and round
my Ego—nothing.   " I make my being depend on
Nothing."   Like the peaks of Maeterlinck's mountains, Stirner's ego wraps itself in Nothing.

It may be said that this affects only the aristocratic
variety of romanticism.   But in romanticism there is
no real aristocracy.   The conception of aristocracy
has a meaning only when its starting-point is objective.   If the things to be made are shoes, the man
who can best make them is the aristocrat—for he is
the " best."   If the thing is to govern the marches,
the Warden of the Marches is a marquis in the same
way that the leader of an army is a duke.   Given
something to be done, men divide themselves into
aristocrats and not-aristocrats according to their
competence ; and the aristocrat in shoemaking is
not an aristocrat in military affairs, and vice versa.
But as the romantic does not base upon things
the superiority or inferiority of men, there is for him
neither aristocracy nor democracy.   Their supermen

are supermen for the same reason that contemporary dukes are dukes—by grace and not by merit.

The creator of Romanticism was Rousseau. He was a democrat. The first sentence of his " Contrat Sociale " says : " Man is born free and he finds himself everywhere in chains." This sentence made the French Revolution. The French Revolution was excellent in so far as it destroyed the subjective rights of the nobility and clergy. Classes that in general did not fulfil any useful social function had not the right to such rights. But the Revolution attempted to substitute for the subjective rights of the few the subjective rights of all, as if an error became a truth by multiplication. It founded them on the principle that " man is born free." But is it true that man is born free? The poor baby ! Is not the enigma the Sphinx set Ædipus more true : What is the animal that first walks on four legs, then on two, then on three? And will you tell me what " to be free " or " to be born free " means? For to be free from headaches means only not to have headaches. And there are many, many men who cannot find in the word " freedom " more than a negative meaning.

There are now thinkers who make of " personal liberties " an " alogical and axiomatic bedrock " and decline " to waste time in discussing it." I am sorry. Only on two " *absolute* alogical bedrocks " can be based the " *relative* alogical bedrock " of liberty. First, on a theory of law and the State founded on the person, as the fountain of rights. Second, on a theory of Ethics, looking to the interior of consciousness as the exclusive source of morality. This subjective theory of Ethics has been upset by a teacher of Cambridge, Mr. G. E. Moore. Now we see the foundations of Ethics not in man but in the good of the good things that our fathers did for us and in the bad of the bad things that our fathers did not remove, but that we *ought* to replace for our sons. As for the personal theory of right, it has been superseded by a professor of Bordeaux, M. Léon Duguit, by another theory based on solidarity, according to which there are no other rights than the rights annexed to the social functions of every man. No functions, no rights ! Mr. Moore is well known in England, M. Duguit is the first name of France in matters of the theory of law, and both are in earnest.

Kant, hallucinated by Rousseau, tried to find a positive theory. To him to be free meant to fulfil the moral law ; and he did not deduce this moral law from the property of goodness possessed by some things and some actions, but he drew it complete out of his own head, and he felt, as he found it there, the same trembling wonder produced in him by the contemplation of the starry heavens above him. " He often made us weep, he shook our hearts like an earthquake, he liberated our spirits often from the chains of selfish hedonism up to the self-consciousness of the pure freedom of the will," wrote his pupil Jachman as he recalled his student years. And it is easy to understand that one can weep with pride on imagining oneself the bearer within of the moral law, autonomous, sovereign, absolute, without need of appeal to history, to example, or to results, but, on the contrary, suppressing every matter and thinking only in the pure form of our practical reason. But it was not so that Plato taught Ethics. For he sought Ethics in good things, actual or desirable ; and to show what virtue is he sketched the Constitution of an ideal republic, and to show a good man he described the death of Socrates.

The romantic spirit begins by persuading us that we are kings. Then it perceives that we have no throne. Then it seeks for the cause of our lack, and it finds it in external obstacles—society, the human body, the nature of the world—and it ends by throwing us against the obstacles. It begins by making us weep in admiration of our own greatness ; it ends by making us weep out of spite at our littleness. It begins by filling us with joy at the discovery of our right to the throne ; it ends by filling us with hatred of our usurpers—Nature, our own pity, or other men. And this is why Romanticism begins in the Humanism of the Renaissance and ends in universal conflagration. For what can men do, if filled with pride, but exterminate one another ?

Classicism, like Romanticism, acknowledges that man is the king of creation. But Classicism adds that man is a servant—the servant of God, the highest good, the highest truth, the highest beauty. As king of creation, man is superior to all other things and to all other animals ; but, on the other hand, he is inferior to the good, the true, and the beautiful. He may use things and animals for his satisfaction ; he ought to serve absolute values. The consciousness of his superiority over things can help man to cure himself of lust. The consciousness of his inferiority with respect to absolute values can help him to cure himself of pride. Lust and pride are the two aspects of original sin. But that has already been said by Pascal, and, before Pascal, by the Fathers of the Church. Classicism is already very old ; but for some centuries it was a class without intelligent pupils. Now Romanticism is dead ; and there are curious souls returning to the class.

THE FAILURE OF LIBERTY

LIBERTY is defended on the pretext that men are happier when they do what they wish. But against that must be said, first, that it is doubtful whether men are happy when they do what they wish ; and, secondly, that we cannot conceive any society which allows men to do what they wish, for it is in the nature of men to wish for impossibilities. The magic of liberty does not belong properly to liberty itself, but to its associations. If the Pope were to prohibit Catholics from reading the Bible to-morrow, or from studying theology for fear that they might become heretics, the faithful would revolt in the name of liberty ; but the sacredness of their revolt would be founded, not upon liberty but upon thought. If the English Government prohibited the exploitation of some of the country's natural resources, the population would revolt in the name of liberty ; but the justification for their revolt would lie, not in liberty but in the fact that the increase of wealth is a good thing. If the Government of any European country decreed that its women should bind up their feet so as to make them smaller, as Chinese women once did, the women would revolt, again in the name of liberty ; but the real reason for their revolt would not be liberty but health or grace.

As man is not an automaton, to deprive him in normal circumstances of the freedom of finding his own vocation or calling among the professions or trades considered as necessary would be to destroy, him, and it would also lead to his destruction if he were obliged to fulfil his function in an automatic manner. It is in these two senses only that personal liberty is not merely, legitimate but necessary ; for no society can subsist for long if it does not adjust itself to the nature of man, which is incompatible with automatism. By that we only declare that all laws must take into account the fact that man is not a machine but a free agent. But it is necessary to be clear on one point, and equally, necessary to emphasize it: that when we defend liberty of thought we are really defending thought itself and not liberty ; for, if we were defending only the principle of liberty, we might find ourselves upholding the cause of not thinking at all. Liberty is not in itself a positive principle of social organization. To speak of a society whose members are at liberty to do as they please is a contradiction in terms. Liberty in this sense would constitute no society at all. The rules of all kinds of societies prescribe that members shall do certain things and shall refrain from doing others. The good that has sometimes been attained in the name of liberty, such as the restriction of authority or the promotion of thought, trade, etc., would have been better attained had we fought straightway for the restriction of authority and for the promotion of thought and trade as such ; and we should have avoided this strange superstition that makes so many men believe that liberty gives them a legitimate right to refuse to fulfil any function necessary to the society to which they belong.

FUNCTION AND VALUES

13

THE RULES OF THE GUILDS: LIMITA-
TION AND HIERARCHY

ROMANTICISM favours the indefinite expansion of individual power. The mediæval Guilds raised against this indefiniteness the two rules of Limitation and Hierarchy. Actuality placed us not long ago before a fact which shows that the spirit of the old Guilds is not entirely dead. But it is the case that the Guilds themselves are dead. What may, then, signify the revival or the resurrection of their spirit? May it not be that the Guilds responded to the vital need of every human society, aspiring to stability? May it not be that there is a natural harmony between the Guild institutions and the ideal of justice, a harmony that could only be broken by a great catastrophe or by great negligence?

Every honest thinker has to confess that even if we could abolish by a stroke of the pen every privilege of inheritance and caste that maintains the exploitation of man by man, not even then should we succeed in building economic society upon solid foundations of justice. We should still be in need of an adjustment between the principles of Liberty and Democracy. By virtue of the Liberal principle every man would develop his economic gifts, and as these are not equal—for instance, those of the man of prey and those of the saint, the artist, or the thinker—the result would be the distribution of economic power to the exclusive advantage of men of economic talent, but in absolute prejudice to the rest of mankind. This may make the usurer smile, but it is an offence to our common humanity. Alternatively, by virtue of the absolute democratic principle, we should level the economic power of every man at the cost of ignoring our fundamental inequality, which denies that the same social power should be given to the head that directs a complex industry as to the arm that carries out passively and indifferently, its direction. Absolute Liberalism contradicts our common humanity, absolute Democracy our obvious inequality.

The Guilds, on the contrary, acknowledge equally the fact of our common humanity and the fact of our differences. The two great principles of the Guild are Limitation and Hierarchy. Limitation says that the humblest of men is, after all, a man and not a beast and must be paid enough to live ; but it adds that the most competent of masters and craftsmen is, finally, not a god, but no more than a man, and has no right but to a limited income: the principle of limitation implies both the maximum and the minimum incomes. Hierarchy divides and subdivides the members of the Guilds into apprentices, craftsmen, and masters. The maintenance of the limitation and the hierarchy was made possible only by an active spirit of rivalry, even of jealousy, that kept every man strictly within the privileges of his standing, and actually shows us to-day a strange resurrection of this spirit of the old Guilds.

For the purpose of studying as a whole the problem of the organization and mobilization of labour for the production of armaments a committee, with seven Trade Union representatives on it, was organized in Newcastle-on-Tyne. This movement means the co-operation of the workmen in the management of industries. In the words of the *Nation*: " The employers have made experiments in scientific management, in long hours, in the seven-day week, in various methods of stimulating and increasing production. What we want is the workman's experience and the workman's judgment." It would now seem as if this suggestion were about to be applied on a small scale. The *Nation* calls this experiment " the new Syndicalism." And, though one would think it ought to be called " Guild Socialism "—because it does not relate to an anonymous idea evoked from the bowels of the earth, but to a plan which has been advocated systematically, in the columns of the *New Age* for years past and has already, been christened in proper form—it is hardly worth while wrangling over words.

The interesting thing is that this movement has arisen because the working classes refused to tolerate the system whereby, a few individuals secured vast profits out of the war. The fact that the workmen found themselves suffering from the increase in the cost of living consequent upon the war certainly helped to bring about the strike which finally led the British Government to intervene with a view to restricting profits in the engineering trade. But the fundamental motive of the action taken by the workers must be sought in the immensity of the profits which the masters had been obtaining previously. On this occasion the workmen did not protest so much against their own poverty as against the wealth of their employers. An enemy, of the working classes might say that this time they, were actuated by jealousy rather than by self-interest. What in reality did move them was the old, the eternal spirit of the Guilds.

Let us not be afraid of the word "jealousy." It is an ugly word and has an ugly meaning when this sadness at another's good is on account of the strictly individual possessions of our neighbour —his talents, his virtues, or his charms. A passion of the soul that cannot be satisfied is a hell without issue. " Jealousy is thin, for it bites and does not eat," carved rather than wrote the Spaniard Quevedo. But when jealousy refers to the material powers—political, economic, military—it is only the psychological mood of the public or republican spirit. The motto of the old Liberals—" The price of liberty is eternal vigilance "—is no more than the organization of this jealousy. A similar device was perhaps inscribed on the dagger of Brutus. But if eternal vigilance is considered necessary in the political world, to guard against the tyranny of magistrates, much more is it necessary in the economic world. The magistrate, after all—king, member of parliament, judge, or general—is tethered to his magistracy, and magistracies are public functions which can only be abused in a public way, and at the risk of public indignation. But the power of money is indirect, and it can work, and does work, secretly its corruption. The Americans took great care to balance nicely in their Constitution the powers of their executive, judicial, and legislative magistrates, but they did not take such pains to restrain economic power. When they awoke from their dream they found that behind their executive, judicial, and legislative powers was only one efficient power: Money.

In a lecture delivered against the Guild idea, Mrs. Sidney Webb discovered that the old guilds did not fix a minimum wage scale, but, on the contrary, a maximum. For Mrs. Webb, apparently, *the* important thing for the workmen was the

Minimum Wage. The idea of limiting wages in particular, or individual earnings in general, should rather have appeared to her to be foreign to the interests of the workmen and of democracy—or, at least, a secondary matter. Mr. Bernard Shaw, too, has often repeated his thesis that all that is wrong with the poor is their poverty, and that their ideal ought to be to get rich. As an epigram it will pass, but Mr. Shaw knows quite well that it is impossible, because poverty and wealth are not absolute concepts, but correlative terms ; and the poverty of the poor will only disappear with the wealth of the wealthy ; for they are the same thing. And though Mrs. Webb and Mr. Shaw, by the very fact that they are Socialists, are enemies of the wealth of the rich, the type of Socialism they profess, State Socialism, does not aim at controlling the power of the powerful.

For it is evident that State Socialism will entirely abolish the wealth of the rich when it establishes the ownership in common of the means of production, distribution, and exchange. But the State which does such a thing will not be, as the idealogues appear to think, a pure entity of reason, but a government, an executive power, a bureaucracy ; and the men who will assume the power under it now possessed by the capitalists will consequently be men of flesh and bone, constituted as a governing class. It is quite possible that, under such a régime, the workers might attain a position of greater security than they now enjoy. But, at bottom, they will have done no more than change their masters and their form of government. The bureaucrats will replace the capitalists ; political power economic power ; the present State will be replaced by the Servile State. The only advantage which the Servile State possesses over the present

State is that, under the former, the incomes of potentates would be limited, exactly as even the Civil Lists of monarchs are limited now. There would, in consequence, be no single individuals commanding the enormous economic power at present wielded by the Rockefellers or the Krupps. But the power of the governing classes under the Servile State would include, as well as their present political power, the economic power now exercised by the capitalists ; and the life of the masses, as at present, would lie at the mercy of a few men.

The reason is that the Guilds alone are capable of limiting the material power of individuals. The limitation of individual power is the characteristic function of the Guilds, as it is of every corporation. Not that the Guilds were egalitarian. The Guilds knew very well that men differed in value, and that their production was unequal in quantity and quality. A Guild organization or a corporation was always modelled on a hierarchical plan. In the Church there were the three orders of deacons, priests, and bishops ; in trades there were the grades of apprentices, craftsmen, and masters. But every hierarchy has taken as much care to limit the power and pay of the inferiors as to limit the maxima of the superiors. The formula by which the noblemen of Aragon elected their king in the Middle Ages is well known: "We, who are as worthy as you, and who together are worthier than you, make you our king that you may guard our privileges and liberties ; and if not, no." Why did the Guilds limit the power of the individuals ? Simply because a non-limitation of power threatens every organization with disaster. The Guild was liable to this fate ; and it was in the Guild that the remaining members found their security and stability.

The Guilds died out precisely because their principle of the limitation of individual power did not succeed in becoming an essential part of the organization of all the other callings. Feudal lords, for instance, were able to exploit and expropriate their peasants. In commerce and money-lending —callings not regulated by the Guild principle— considerable blocks of capital in money were formed during the Middle Ages. To this there was added later the capital resulting from the discovery of gold and silver mines in America, and the slave labour of the natives of America and Africa. On the one hand the feudal lords kept on throwing into the towns such vast hordes of labourers that the Guilds could not assimilate them ; on the other hand, capitalists, formed by usury and foreign trade, exploited these workmen in new factories built close to the sea, on open land, beyond the control of the cities and their Guild institutions. Hence, in England, the bitter struggle provoked between the corporate towns and the new industries, which ended in the rout of the Guilds and in the triumph of capitalism, with all its horrors. That is to say, the Guilds perished because side by side with them a new economic power sprang into existence which the Guilds could not control. But they would have perished long before if their regulations had permitted their masters to enrich themselves, for those masters would have become capitalists exploiting the work of the craftsmen and apprentices. The ruin of the Guilds did not come about because they limited the power of their members, but because the Guilds did not succeed in bringing agricultural production into the Guild system, and also because they were even less able to subject the exploitation of undeveloped countries to Guild control.

Even in this temporary death of the Guilds can

be discerned the wisdom of their principle. What was wrong with the Guilds was that they failed to realize the danger their own life ran by the development of unlimited power not subject to their control. Their internal constitution was good, for it was inspired by a spirit of " balance of power " among their own members. It was only their short-sightedness which led the Guilds to perish. As well as a domestic policy, they should have had a foreign policy, based likewise on the principle of balance of power. Even at this moment there are Englishmen who would like to see their country holding aloof from continental struggles, and who express the utmost horror at the principle of the " balance of power." But this principle has saved England. How would England have benefited from saving her expenditure on the present war if, by her abstention, she had permitted to develop on the other side of the North Sea a Germany so powerful that her mere wish would have resulted in the realization of her ambitions? In this world there are no isolated forces. Every material human force which is formed behind our back will one day meet us face to face.

That is why the Clyde engineers have done well, not merely in taking care to improve their own position, but in protesting against the excessive profits of their masters. Capital that accumulates in other hands than those which produce it may to-morrow be utilized against the interests of the workers, exactly as the capital at the disposal of the usurers and the exploiters of overseas countries was turned against the Guilds. The profits which Government contractors are now pocketing will be used to-morrow to build in China factories whose products will lower the price of goods in the world-market, and consequently the wages of workmen in Europe. It is not sufficient that the workmen shall rest content with improving their own position ; they must also see to it that no power arises elsewhere which to-morrow may threaten their interests.

God grant that the example of the Clyde and Newcastle may be followed as soon as possible in other professions. In none is more urgent the restoration of the Guild spirit than in our artistic and intellectual professions. Perhaps it is because the evil kind of jealousy, the jealousy of merit, is so intense amongst us that we have allowed to fall asleep the holy jealousy of power and success and have consented to the creation of a state of things all over the world in which success is almost synonymous with fraud. An unscrupulous barrister may make hundreds of thousands by juggling with the articles of the law, while a man who reveals and clarifies with years of labour and inspiration the principles of the Constitution may be unable to find a publisher to produce his book except at his own expense. The most eminent living musician, the head of his profession, the composer Sir Edward Elgar, may earn no more than the wages of an artisan, while many prima donnas become millionaires. There is not material sustenance in the modern world either for original thinking or for creative art, but the whole planet is the pedestal of the virtuoso, the impresario, the low comedian, the pornographist, the paradoxist, and the flatterer of the idle rich or of the mob. Would that be possible if the standing and income of every member were fixed by the artistic and intellectual Guilds ?

WAR AND SOLIDARITY

THE Guild spirit can rise again in its entirety only if the consciousness of the solidarity of men in economic effort is strengthened and enlightened. Will the war help towards this? In my judgment Yes, for these reasons: (1) The war has compelled nations to overcome all kinds of subjective rights which form barriers in the way of human solidarity. Among these subjective rights are, for instance, private property, and all rights arising from privilege and private contracts. The principle of *salus populi* is not the *suprema lex*, but war makes it justly supreme over private property. (2) The war has revived the spirit of brotherhood in arms. There is no higher form of peace than this spirit of brotherhood in a cause believed to be just. The idea of peace cannot be separated from that of war. The greeting *Pax vobis* means " Peace to you who are fighting against evil." Brotherhood in arms is peace in war. And peace without war is unthinkable. I do not say that it is not possible that in the future there may not be a way superior to this of defeating the Germans, although I believe that this is good enough for the time being. What I say is that war must be eternal, universal, and obligatory so long as evil lasts. (3) War enlightens the concept of solidarity. It does not create a direct solidarity among men, but solidarity in a thing, in a problem, in a common task, in the defence of the national life and territory against the enemy. (4) The great modern armies exemplify, in themselves the spirit and the rules of the Guilds. What differentiates a Guild from an ordinary Trade Union? That in a Trade Union the solidarity of the members is direct ; its object is purely mutual protection. But the members of a Guild are associated in one thing, in a function: railways, mercantile marine, mining, or agriculture. From this thing they receive, like the army from the national defence, their discipline, their dignity, and their internal rules of compulsory work, limitation of pay, and hierarchy, of functions.

When the war is over Europe will be poor. And it is true that the position of the wealthy classes will not be what it was, since their taxes will be heavily increased ; but it is probable that the politicians will hardly succeed in convincing the people of the necessity for maintaining the same type of social order, or disorder, as prevailed in Europe up to the outbreak of war. And they will not succeed because the conscience of Europe will have definitely risen superior to the ideas which governed the world in August 1914. Up to that time economic society was based on the principle of contract. By virtue of this principle the world's wealth belonged to those individuals who could show by legal documents or contracts that they, had a right to it, no matter what their merits or their social services might be. And, although the moral spirit of man has always denied to individuals the right to own wealth not conferred upon them by society as payment for their services, the principle of contract was maintained for reasons of expediency or metaphysical reasons. For reasons of expediency, it is maintained by those who say, that the stimulus of property "transforms sand into gold," and that men work, above all, that their children may not be poor. It is useless to say that sand is not transformed into gold, that the spirit of work is not founded on property, but on hunger, and that the industry of the fathers does not justify the parasitism of the sons. For metaphysical reasons this principle of property is defended, not only, by those who see in it a Divine institution, like Grotius, or a natural right, like Hegel, but also, though unconsciously, by those socialistic masses who, deceived by the fatalistic and fantastic philosophy of history of Karl Marx, see in capitalism a fact which is above and external to the consent of the human conscience.

Metaphysics aside, the principle of property based on contract can call to its defence only reasons of expediency. From a moral point of view it cannot be justified ; and the only people who can defend it are those lawyers whose moral spirit is buried in the letter of their legal texts. The law may swear to us that a certain group of shareholders are the proprietors of a manufactory. But our reason tells us that the only people who have a right to it are those who work there with their heads or hands. No lawyers could be found to defend property in the name of the right possessed by dead fathers to transmit to their children the wealth society allowed them to accumulate ; and, if there were such lawyers, they, would be answered in the words used by Thomas Paine to Edmund Burke when the latter, at the time of the French Revolution, denied to nations the right to choose their own rulers: " That which a whole nation chooses to do, it has a right to do. Mr. Burke says, No. Where, then, does the right exist? I am contending for the rights of the *living* and against their being willed away, and controlled and contracted for, by the manuscript assumed authority

of the dead ; and Mr. Burke is contending for
the authority of the dead over the rights and freedom of the living." The fact that Paine was a
pamphleteer rather than a thinker does not make
his argument the less right ; it is for the living
and not the dead to *honour* the services of each
citizen according to his *merits*, and to *pay* for them
according to the needs of the *function* he fulfils.

But this principle was recognized by the conscience of humanity long before the war. Why,
then, did people tolerate the continuance of the
principle whereby wealth was distributed according
to contracts which perpetuated the parasitism of a
few social classes and the servitude of the majority?
At bottom, simply because experience had not yet
refuted with the necessary emphasis the argument
that property was the greatest stimulus to industry.
But the war has made clear the falsity of this argument. Before it broke out it was thought right
that the railways should be managed by their owners,
or by directors nominated by them, entirely in their
own interests. Since the war the interests of the
railways have been subordinated to the interests of
the nation. Before the war it seemed to be right
that the wealthy classes should invest their superfluous money wherever they liked. Now the
Government has prohibited the export of capital,
since it is wanted for the war. Before the war
merchants traded freely ; now, under severe
penalties, they are forbidden to trade with enemy
countries. Further, the Government assumed powers
for taking over whatever factories it deemed
advisable for the manufacture of war munitions ;
and it also imposed a special tax on war profits.
Public utility comes first, contract or no contract.
Even individuals cannot escape from the range of
this principle. The belligerent nations soon learned

that it was not moral, and in certain cases indeed
not lawful, for individuals to deny their aid to the
work of the whole.   The universal mobilization of
labour is being discussed in England.   The rumour
will become a reality if the necessities of the war
render it essential for every citizen to play his part.
Then we shall see established the principle that
every man and woman, rich or poor, must take
his   share   in   the   common   task,   fulfilling   such
functions as may be thought necessary.   And this
principle will have triumphed, not only because it
is moral, but also because it is more advantageous
to the State than the principle which permits individual contracts to decide the wealth and status of
people.

The war, however, will not only have proved
that the principle of contract, beneficial though it
may be for some individuals, is not the most
advantageous for society, but it will in addition
have created the spirit of solidarity necessary for
effecting, without excessive violence, the transformation of a society, founded on the false right of
a few individuals to parasitism, into another society,
a society based on the recognition of the principle
of solidarity, by virtue of which no one can have
rights who has not fulfilled his duties.   Many men
who, in times of peace, did nothing but sign
cheques, play bridge, and go on motor tours, are
now rubbing down horses in camp, or acting as
sentries, or exposing themselves to the enemy's
shrapnel in the trenches.   Many society women,
the Countess of Warwick tells us, are now spending their time in hospitals or in workshops, working
even harder than they would expect their own maids
to do.   Most of these people are satisfied with
their new life.   They have found in social service
what they lacked in their former existence: the

feeling of reality. And, now that they have once felt themselves ennobled by work, would not they blush if, after the peace, they were condemned to do nothing more than impose upon the poor the unnecessary task of attending to their luxuries?

It would be too much, nevertheless, to hope that a social transformation could be effected by the spontaneous conversion of the privileged classes. Social changes are carried out when the oppressed realize that they can become strong by union and enthusiasm. And the democracies of Europe have not lost consciousness of their power during the war. The fact that the war has blown to the winds the international pacifism of the older Socialist does not mean that it has destroyed the principle of social solidarity which is the essential part of Socialism. It has strengthened it. The consciousness of power is never so intense among the people as when they defend by force of arms a cause which is dear to them ; and the cause of nationality is dear to each of the countries fighting for it, and the cause of humanity to those who are going to win. In peace time the workman in a factory sees no more meaning in his labour than that he is earning his wages. He now knows that with every shell he makes he is helping to maintain the immortality of his nation, as much as the man who faces the enemy's fire. Both classes learn, in war time, the great lesson that success depends upon the co-ordination of the effort of each individual in the common effort.

War is a lesson in solidarity. Rich and poor disappear in the brotherhood of arms. In the organization of armies the position of individuals is not fixed by contracts but by the function they fulfil. The rewards of war are not based on contracts but on services rendered. The separation

14

of governors and governed is not effected in war
in fulfilment of the will of the dead, as in the
separation of rich and poor in times of peace, but
by the differentiation of functions which everybody
realizes as necessary. In this sense war is a lesson
in discipline ; but the discipline is founded on the
evidence that the ruled fulfils less difficult functions
than the ruler. War teaches men to respect merit
more profoundly—and not merely the merits of
soldiers, but all technical abilities. Before the war
there was a great deal of talk in England of protecting research and inventions more carefully. But
it is the war which has shown the need of increasing
the number of chemists, electricians, civil engineers.
The competent " captain of industry " is not less
respected than before, but more. War has cured
the workers of their old exclusivism. But the idle
rich man is no longer admired as of old ; and
the same remark applies to the cosmopolitan
financier, the clever lawyer, and the intellectual who
devotes his ingenuity to confusing truth with
falsehood.

It is not conceivable that, after having learned
in war to face death and to exert their will, the
workmen of Europe can return to the apathy which
resigned them to economic injustice perpetrated by
stamped paper, at a time when their reason had
been won over to the principle of social solidarity.
It is not likely that, after a shock so deep as war,
the workmen will return to their factories and pay
for the campaign out of their reduced wages in
order that shareholders may come quietly back to
their old idle existence. The war is awakening,
in millions of brains, nervous cells which had long
been asleep. Men are learning in the Army, for
example, that the greatest efforts and sacrifices of
which men are capable are not called forth by love

of money, but by the spirit of honour and by the Guild spirit. Every army is a guild in which, in the hour of danger, the whole nation incorporates itself.

Every human expedient is born of necessity. Some disappear with necessity, others remain. Those that remain are the instruments of the permanent values of culture. The splints for a broken arm are discarded when the arm is healed ; but the stopping of a broken tooth is retained. Every religion is probably born as a necessity of tribal coherence, that of Babylon as well as that of Israel. The Babylonian dies to be of interest only to Assyriologists, but the Israelite remains for its ethical spirit in all Islam and Christendom. Necessity gives to the human consciousness the situation of fact in which it must find its basis for its expediencies ; but it is only when these expediencies serve permanent values that they endure when they have ceased to be strict necessities. The economic spirit is brought into existence by penury, but does not die with it. Nor does the solidarity which war enkindles die with war. Solidarity was an ethical value long before the war ; it is the war which has made it expedient. But it is its positive and permanent value which will make it survive the necessity that has brought it forth.

THE DOCTRINE OF OBJECTIVE RIGHTS

THE spirit of solidarity is a vague thing. It cannot triumph if it is not expressed in a legal formula. But the legal formula of a new social system cannot be improvised. The declaration of the Rights of Man in 1789 would not have been possible if Rousseau had not published his "Social Contract" in 1762. Nor would it be possible to establish in the immediate future a society based on the principle of No function no rights, if this principle had not previously been formulated. But it has been formulated by Duguit. The difference between the eighteenth and the twentieth century is this: While in the eighteenth century, in spite of illiteracy, the books of Rousseau and of Tom Paine were read by the hundred thousand, there is no Syndicalist, so far as I know, who has read the books of the theorist Duguit. The multiplication of silly books and silly newspapers has stultified, among the general public, all sense of intellectual values.

M. Léon Duguit, Professor of Constitutional Law in the University of Bordeaux, has destroyed the subjective conception of Law and created instead an objective conception, as the juridical basis of a syndicalist, functionarist, or Guild society which he believes will, in a short time, be called upon to take the place of societies as they exist at present —founded as these are, like that of ancient Rome, on the two conceptions of the State and of private property, the *Imperium* and the *Dominium*.

All other jurists continue to base Law and Rights on subjective conceptions because they are still fascinated by the problem of Austin—the problem of " where supreme power ultimately resides." In this way they come to see in Law nothing but a command from sovereignty. You are already familiar with the doctrine of Austin. I give below the summary by Mr. Sidgwick in his " Elements of Politics."

" Every positive law of any State is a general command to do or abstain from certain acts which is issued directly or indirectly by the Sovereign of the State to a person or persons subject to his authority ; the sovereign being that determinate person, or body of persons combined in a certain manner, that the bulk of the members of the State habitually obey, provided he or it does not habitually obey any one else." " From this definition two consequences are inferred : (*a*) the power of the Sovereign cannot be legally limited ; (*b*) sovereignty cannot, strictly speaking, be legally divided between two or more persons, or bodies of persons acting separately."

You know also the objections which destroy Austin's theory. They were formulated by Mr. Sidgwick in two questions : " Where, then, in England is the Sovereign with power free from ' legal limitations ' ? " " Is it the House of Commons, or is it the body of enfranchised Englishmen that periodically elects its Members ? Austin shrinks from the paradox of affirming the former, which would compel him to view the Government of England as an extremely narrow oligarchy ; he cannot consistently affirm the latter, since it is obvious that no command of the electorate as such has any legal force." Mr. Dicey is trying to solve the dilemma by a dual application of the term "Sovereignty," saying that Parliament is the *legal* Sovereign and the electorate the *political* Sovereign ; but this conception of a double sovereignty destroys fundamentally the thesis put forward by Austin (and by Rousseau and Hobbes as well) that only one sovereignty is possible within a State.

Mr. Sidgwick, however, is ceaselessly occupied with the problem of finding out where the public power actually resides, as if this were a juridical question. He does not see that the question of supreme authority is purely a question of power, and that questions of power are not really juridical at all, but merely questions of fact. There are some individuals and social classes which have more power than others. The power of individuals and of social classes is continually changing. In the year 1906, for example, the Parliament of Great Britain had more power than it has now, and the Cabinet had less. This transference of power has not been due to any law ; it is merely a fact which the observer takes note of and investigates. To the question "Where does supreme power reside?" the jurist is unable to provide any answer. It is only the historian who can tell us where the power of commanding lies at any given moment. Power is simply a fact. So far as its origin is concerned, no power is legitimate.

As the doctrine of representative power falls to the ground because we do not know finally whether power lies with Parliament or with the electorate, the German jurists (Gierke, Jellinek, etc., and, in England, Green) have tried to replace this by the organic theory. They start from the postulate that corporations are juridical persons, and consequently capable, like individuals, of becoming subjective agents of Law. But as juridical persons must possess will to create or to exercise rights, and as will is to be found only in individuals, it follows that it is only individuals who express the will of collective persons, thus serving them as *organs*. The State is a corporate and indivisible person, the only nominal possessor of public power. Rulers, officials, nations, parliaments, and chiefs of the State are the individuals who express the will of the State. It is not they who create and execute ; it is the State who, through them, creates and executes. M. Duguit destroys the German organic theory merely by saying that it leads to the same insoluble dilemma as the Anglo-French theory of representative power. " Is the will of the State that which exists through its organs? or is it the organs which exist by the will of the State? "

This Gordian knot is cut by M. Duguit with his objective theory of Law. Instead of asking who makes the Law and by what right, M. Duguit inquires what sort of thing Law is : what Law is in itself. He answers his questions by saying that " men are under a social rule based upon the interdependence which unites them." This rule must exist. If its basis is challenged, M. Duguit would not hesitate to postulate it. The interdependence of men being taken for granted, there arises the necessity for rules of conduct which must be imposed upon everybody. With this definition the problem of sovereignty disappears. Social necessity creates laws. If a group of men wish to amuse themselves by playing football, the first thing necessary is to draw up laws of football and then to nominate referees who will cause them to be respected—or perhaps the most competent to do so will nominate themselves as referees. From the strictly juridical point of view all this is a matter of indifference. The law of football arises from the fact that men who wish to play football are mutually interdependent. Nobody has any subjective right to impose a law—neither the majority nor the minority, nor the State itself, nor the nation, nor a collectivity, nor the individuals, nor the nobles, nor the plebeians, nor the capitalists, nor the proletariat, nor the citizens, nor the social classes. Social rules exist because without them society itself could not exist, and these social rules are disciplinary because every society is in itself a discipline. The social rule is based upon solidarity, and solidarity on the fact of men's interdependence, "which unites by community of needs and by the division of work the members of humanity, and especially members of the same social group." M. Duguit's idea is, as we see, classical. Remember the words in which Plato founds his city : " A city takes its rise from this, that none of us happens to be self-sufficient, but is indigent of many things " (" Republic," 369).

This social rule is juridical and not merely ethical, because it regulates only the external conduct of man, and not his inward desires or wishes, and because it imposes on men only those acts which possess some social value, and so far as they are of this value and produce a social effect. It is not an absolute rule such as those prescribed by natural law, but which change with the different types of life presented to us by different human societies. It is not the basis of subjective right either for the individual "because of the pre-eminent human dignity," to use the phrase of the French jurist, M. Michel, or for the State, on account of the traditional prestige of the regal powers in it. According to this rule there are no subjective rights, but only objective rights which are " the social obligations upon everybody to carry out a certain mission, and the power of performing the actions necessitated by the fulfilment of this mission." M. Duguit takes as his own the phrase of Comte : "No one has any other right than that of always doing his duty."

The reason why the theory of subjective rights has lasted for so long is ascribed by M. Duguit to the fact that the Roman jurists had reinvested it with the double armour of the *imperium* and the *dominium*. The *imperium* is, like the Sovereign of Austin and Rousseau, the subjective right of commanding—the absolute, indivisible right which exists by itself without any other reason than that of being the public power. M. Duguit flatly denies the existence of public power as a juridical concept. Clearly enough he recognizes the existence of individuals who command by the fact that they are more powerful than others ; but this fact of the governing force does not need to be explained by a belief in the existence of a sovereign substance, as the personality of the nation or of the individual or of the State. The existence of this sovereign substance is a hypothesis which is affirmed, but is not, and cannot be, proved because it is a purely metaphysical and scholastic formula, "like that of the individual soul, the reflecting substance and its faculties." Nor, in M. Duguit's view, does the collective will exist. The only will is that of individuals. "A law is voted by 10,000 citizens and is imposed by them on 5,000 more," but neither the power of the number nor the quality of the individuals can create the subjective right to command. The *imperium* is an indefensible myth. Nobody has any right to command because he is superior to others. He commands because he exercises more power, or in fulfilment of the mission which the law entrusts to him. In the first case the command is a fact ; in the second case it is a juridical fact, but in no case does the *imperium* exist as a subjective right.

By the *dominium* the Romans wished to make over in favour of certain individuals the absolute power to dispose of a given quantity of wealth, and of imposing on all other people respect for this power. It was an absolute right which included the rights of enjoyment, use, and disposal, and went even beyond death. But this subjective right is also another metaphysical conception which is already disappearing from the juridical sphere.

M. Duguit does not make this statement because he is an enemy of private property. He does not tell us that individual property is going to disappear. He even affirms the right of existence of a pure capitalistic class entrusted with the task of collecting the savings of one generation and utilizing them to prepare the working capital for the following generation. What M. Duguit does deny is that such a capitalistic class has any subjective right to property, and, on the other hand, he does affirm its social mission. " Property ceases to be an individual right, and is turned instead into a social function." " As long as the capitalist class fulfils the mission assigned to it, it will live. When it abandons this mission it will disappear as the clergy and the nobility disappeared in 1789."

We may sum up M. Duguit's theory by saying that it radically denies that the law is an order of command. " It is a discipline of fact which social interdependence imposes on every member of the group." But how can it be proved that the law is not an order? Because an order does not apply to those who give it, and the law does. If the law were an order, one could not explain the fact that Members of Parliament remain subject to a law which they themselves have voted. The Germans have tried to explain this fact by inventing the theory of self-limitation, " by virtue of which, when the State self-limits itself, it self-determines itself and persists as Sovereign, although subject to its own law." But this is merely playing with words or conceptions, because to say that the State binds itself to itself as it wishes, and because it may wish, is equivalent to saying that it does not bind itself at all. On the other hand, when it is denied that laws are the expression of the individual will of Members of Parliament, and when it is said, further, that they can be imposed only when they are the formulation of the rules of Law, and in the measure that they are so, then their universal and obligatory character is explained.

It may be objected to M. Duguit's theory that his rule of Law will be obeyed only in so far as the individuals who monopolize power may wish to obey it. Certainly. But M. Duguit himself does not deny this. If to-day there were individuals in possession of as much power as Herod, they might order the massacre of the innocents or they could, at any rate, evade every social rule which might hamper them. But the massacre of the innocents is not an example of a juridical order, but of arbitrary power. And, so far as its realization is concerned, the whole theory of M. Duguit is based on the contemporary fact of the syndicalist movement, which is leading to the result that " the power of Governments must necessarily diminish day by day, and become at length reduced to the power of vigilance and interference alone ; for all the economic functions are gradually being distributed among the different social classes, which are acquiring, through the development of syndicalism, a definite juridical structure." Thus the objective theory of law comes to be, in M. Duguit's system, the *juridical* basis of a syndicalist, functionarist, or Guild society. And, on the other hand, the development of the syndicalist, functionarist, or Guild movement forms the *historical* basis which converts into reality the objective doctrine of right. Let the reader be aware that in this system there is no vicious circle. An objective conception of right leads us not to believe in other rights than those of the function which men carry out. But only the increase of functionarist corporations, such as Trade Unions, Law Societies, Medical Associations, etc., can inspire the objective doctrine with the breath of life.

Hence M. Duguit is led to plead that there may be constituted " a high tribunal, composed of equal representatives of every social class, which shall judge, if we may so put it, of the legality of laws," and he goes on to express the hope that the society of the coming generations may resemble that which feudalism, " after many violent fights and struggles, created in the thirteenth century— a society, incidentally very cosmopolitan, in which social classes, hierarchized and co-ordinated, were united to one another by a system of conventions which acknowledged in them a series of reciprocal rights and duties, with the intervention of the King, the superior Sovereign, entrusted (to use the fine phrase of the period) with making prevail ' order and peace through justice '—that is to say, with ensuring, on the part of each group, the fulfilment of those duties imposed on it by its place in the social structure."

THE LEGAL PRINCIPLES OF THE
HUMAN COMMONWEALTH

LET us see how the objective doctrine of Law may offer an adequate solution to international problems.

Either the Germans will win or they will not. If they do win, the other nations will be able to think of nothing for the next hundred years but demolishing the world-wide Empire which the Germans will' establish, or preventing them from establishing it as the consequence of this first victorious stage. That means that the twentieth century, will devote itself exclusively to conspiring against Germany. If the Germans do not win, the balance of power in Europe will be re-established in one form or another.

We shall assume that the balance of power has been restored. We may likewise assume that the belligerent countries will do their best to maintain the balance. They will be interested, above all, in preserving peace. The lesson of the war will not be forgotten in one or two generations—there will be too many dead. Even without any other international agreements than the treaty of peace, the countries will all do their best to maintain the *status quo* resulting from the war itself.

But before peace is broken again the countries will realize that the *status quo* cannot be maintained indefinitely. The reason? Very simple. The *status quo* is static by definition, and life is dynamic. Ten years after the treaty of peace has been signd some nations will be observed to ascend, to regenerate; others to fall, to degenerate. In the former ambition will rise again ; in the latter, fear. This is inevitable, even if the treaty of peace limits armaments. The military strength of a country does not consist only in its army and navy, but in its population, its metallurgical industries, in the totality of its resources, in the spirit of its sons.

Remembering the horrors of this war, the countries will try to secure themselves against the possibility that the ambition of some and the fear of others will lead to their repetition. That is to say, they will seek a way of solving international difficulties by means of law and not by means of force. That was the thought which inspired the two Hague Conferences. Therefore there will be a third Conference at The Hague or elsewhere. And an attempt will be made to avoid the errors which led to the failure of the first two. But, whether a third Peace Conference is held or not, as soon as there are signs that the new *status quo* is changing, the remembrance of the war will urge the countries to try and solve their disputes by means of law.

But here begins the problem. There are simple-minded pacifists who still hope to find the solution in universal and compulsory arbitration. And to a certain extent they are right. If nations agree to submit all their disputes to arbitration, there is no doubt that wars will be avoided. We know their reasoning. It runs thus : If it has been found possible to suppress duelling in England, why cannot war be suppressed? Why not?

The simple-minded militarist replies : The reason why disputes between individuals can be settled by juridical means ·lies in the fact that there is a supreme authority, that of the State, which compels individuals to contain themselves within the barriers of legality. Disputes between States cannot be settled in the same way, because States are supreme sovereignties which only of their own free will may, if they like, submit their disputes to arbitration. As there is no authority superior to that of the State, legality is optional for States but obligatory for individuals.

This reply will not do. We are reasoning precisely on the supposition that States *will* recognize in the international court an authority superior to their own, because they wish at any cost to avoid war. And there is no doubt that if they transfer their sovereignty to the Hague Tribunal wars will be avoided in future.

The real objection to this is that States will not blindly transfer their sovereignty to the arbitral court, just as we individuals have not blindly transferred our sovereignty to the ordinary courts. The judges are not arbiters who decide our disputes according to their own lights. Judges are not arbiters ; they are simply functionaries entrusted with the duty of applying the laws, and of solving our disputes according to the laws. Without the law to which it is subjected the authority of the judge is tyranny, and perhaps the worst of tyrannies. Before we can hope that an arbitral court will solve international questions by means of law, we must create international law. First, the thing, the law ; then the men, the judges, the authorities.

Law is a thing which arises from another thing : the solidarity of men in the same thing. Such is the objective doctrine of law. The girls of the village go at sunset to fill their buckets at the well ; and as they cannot all fill them at the same time they have to establish the rule of taking their places in turn. This rule is the law. If doubts arise as to its right interpretation in particular cases, the girls may solve them by themselves ; or, if it seem more convenient to them, they may entrust some person with the duty instead. This person is the authority. The law is essential, the authority accidental. Such is the objective doctrine of law. As opposed to this, the subjective doctrine asserts that law is a command from sovereignty, and that the sovereign is the person or group of persons possessing the power of commanding the others. To which we may reply that historically this may be so, but that it is so neither logically nor morally. Historical truth is a fact, but a fact is not a right. And we shall add that if, to the inducements which the possession of power offers to all men, we further join that of regarding it as the sole legitimate fountain of law, we shall no longer be able to wonder why men kill one another by the million for the sake of the right to command others. But it is precisely this which it is sought to avoid in the future. In order to avoid it, let us try to create international law.

You may tell me that this law has already been created. But that is questionable. Nowadays there are treaties and conventions signed by different States at The Hague and elsewhere. But these treaties are not laws any more than contracts drawn up between private individuals are laws ; since such contracts are valid only when they are legal—that is, when there is a law above them which decides as to their validity. The objective doctrine of law does not believe that law is based on contract, not even on the social contract. It asserts, on the contrary, that the validity of contracts arises from their adjustment to the laws. Contracts, by themselves, are nothing but acts of individual will, which may be annulled by other acts of individual will. International treaties are not international law, except in the sense that they are external signs of the solidarity of all men on our planet earth. They indicate the existence of an unwritten law, but they do not declare it. The States sign them because they are guided, as Poincaré says that geometricians are guided in their discoveries, by the obscure instinct of a more profound geometry that lies at the bottom of things.

In the midst of war we affirm human solidarity. War itself is a proof of solidarity. War is the punishment which follows the transgression of human solidarity. But we are trying to find the legal principles in which human solidarity may be expressed. Can we assert that these principles are expressed in international treaties? Have we any right to hope that international disputes can be settled by means of law if we granted to an arbitral court the power of making respect for treaties obligatory; or if all the neutral Powers, as Mr. Roosevelt wishes, were to decide, without giving up their sovereignty, to impose respect for treaties on the disputing Powers? Such is the problem of Hague Conferences and of international law.

Our reply is in the negative. If an arbitral court judged international conflicts in accordance with treaties, humanity would be condemned to an eternal *status quo*. Poland, for instance, would always be enslaved since the existing treaties enslave her. An international law based exclusively on treaties would make present frontiers eternal. The dominating Powers would be eternally dominating, the dominated countries eternally dominated. Such a juridical system would be the *lasciate ogni speranza* of the oppressed peoples. War itself is more violent but less unjust than such an abominable aspiration.

This idea is not only evil; it constitutes logically a vicious circle. For we have seen that international conflicts arise chiefly because the course of history, with the growth of some countries and the decay of others, alters the *status quo*. Life breaks the *status*

15

quo—and you are trying to mend the breakage with the very *status quo* broken by life ! That is not to attempt to solve international problems by means of law ; it is to ignore them. Thus we explain the failure of the first two Hague Conferences.

But why has this attempt to solve international problems by means of treaties failed? Does not this imply the failure of every attempt to make law prevail in international relations? Let the reader note that law has not failed. What has failed is one conception of law. Treaties are acts of individual will concerted by sovereign States. What has failed in their case is law founded on sovereignty, and consequently on the subjective conception of law. Their failure does not imply the failure of law. There still remains to be tried the application of the objective conception of law to international disputes.

Let us see now whether it will draw us out of the mire. The historical supposition on which the possibility of its application is based consists in the fact that the present war has re-established the balance of power, and that the peoples ardently desire to avoid a repetition of such massacres. Without this stimulus the States will not appeal to the objective doctrine of law. The path to the good is not usually found until we have first lost ourselves in all the others. You know the essential formula of the new doctrine. It says that human rights arise from human functions. A woman acquires rights when she has given birth to a child, a man when he works at something useful. No functions, no rights. If I wished to irritate the philanthropists (by the way, why do they not call themselves " philanthropoids "? What they like in man is that simian part of him which enjoys eating, drinking, and pleasure. But man might be defined as the only animal capable of dying and of killing for an idea. And with this nobler side of man the philanthropists, as a rule, do not feel the slightest sympathy.)—if I wished to irritate the philanthropists I should say that the man who does not work at something useful or good has no right to earth, water, air, or fire, and cannot complain before the courts if another man tramples upon him. But this phrase is paradoxical. For in a society where the objective conception of law prevails, it will not be permissible to trample even on useless people ; but that will not be done in the name of the rights of the useless, but in the name of mercy, which is also a good according to the principles of objective morality.

According to the objective conception of law, neither sovereignty nor the power of the State is anything but an historical fact, which comes to be juridical only when it is exercised in accordance with the law. No man has any right to anything. Nor has any State a right to anything. The rights of States arise from the functions they fulfil. When the war ends, a treaty will be signed fixing the frontiers of the belligerents. This is a mere fact, which will become juridical only when the functions which the States must fulfil in the territories under their jurisdiction are also fixed, and in so far as they fulfil them. To the objective doctrine of law the exclusive source of international law, as of private and public law, is the function.

Please do not say that the State cannot be compared to the individual because the State is a complex of functions. The individual is also a complex of functions. A shoemaker has rights as a shoemaker, but also as a father and as a ratepayer. He has as many rights as social functions—no more and no fewer. But the same thing ought to happen in the case of the State. To submit States to objective law is no more difficult than to submit individuals. But both will submit themselves only when they realize that they must submit themselves to avoid greater evils.

In the same way, as no man has a subjective right to anything, so also has a State no subjective right to govern a territory. The sovereignty and powers of the State are juridical only, when they fulfil necessary functions for the conservation and increase of human solidarity in the planet earth and in cultural values. This is the central principle of the objective conception of law. From it are derived the norms which, in general terms, have to condition or legalize the sovereignty and powers of States.

According to the first norm the territory of each State is a road for the men of other States. By virtue of this norm the States would be obliged to keep their roads open. This would mean, not merely the duty of looking after the railways, the highroads, the rivers, harbours, canals, and lighthouses, but also the duty of maintaining public order, attending to sanitation, and permitting foreigners equality of conditions in trade. In the last result this might lead to the establishment of a system of free trade, or at least of fair trade, all over the world. Let it be observed that the principle is not new. The principle by virtue of which the French justified their conquest of Morocco and the Italians their conquest of Tripoli was that the Moors and the Arabs would not keep their roads open.

According to the second norm every nation ought to exploit " economically " the territory assigned to it. As the surface of the earth is limited, it is not just that one nation should monopolize a considerable part of it without drawing from it all the foodstuffs and raw materials needed by humanity. I do not mean by that expression that the rulers of the vaster territories, such as Russia, Brazil, or Australia, should be ordered, at twenty-four hours' notice, to exploit their lands with the same intensity as Belgium and Lombardy are cultivated. But they should be compelled to show a certain annual average rate of progress in production and population as the price of their sovereignty. The norm of international law would be the same as that which Stuart Mill wished to apply to private property in land : " Whenever, in any country, the proprietor, generally speaking, ceases to be the improver, political economy has nothing to say in defence of landed property, as there established."

And, according to the third norm, every Government would be obliged to treat men as the possible bearers of cultural values. This presupposes the obligation of giving each of them a minimum of education ; of preventing their exploitation by other men ; of not setting obstacles in the way of the performance of their legitimate functions ; and of organizing each society in such a way that it would contribute positively to the conservation and increase of the cultural goods of the world.

The difficulty of applying these norms is immense. I have only outlined them with the full consciousness that it would be absurd to pretend to solve the problems of the world in a few paragraphs. The important thing is to fix the details, and this will require the collaboration of many investigators in every country. But what I do assert is that if international law were constituted on the functional or objective principle, the authority or arbitral tribunal entrusted with the duty of applying it would have at its command an instrument which would permit it to solve international conflicts by juridical means, thus overcoming the present contradiction between the statism of treaties and the dynamism of life.

This tribunal could decide, for example, that a

nation such as Poland should be entitled to become a State when it showed capacity for exploiting its territories, keeping up its roads, and co-operating in the universal culture ; it could compel those States now governing non-autonomous peoples to prepare them for the exercise of sovereignty through a pedagogy of backward races ; and it could solve territorial conflicts between nations with a growing population and nations with a stationary or declining population in favour of the former.

It might happen that States prejudiced by international law would refuse in the name of their rights to accept its decrees. As witness to their belief in their rights men are now killing one another by the million ; and if they wish to continue killing one another I do not see any way of preventing them. I do not say that it is an easy thing to submit either individuals or States to objective law. What I do say is that if they do not so submit themselves the present catastrophe will happen again ; for the objective conception of law is the only one which provides a juridical solution of international conflicts.

Neither do I affirm that the triumph of this doctrine indicates absolutely the end of the use of physical force in disputes between States. At present men are killing one another in order that States may acquire territory in which to exercise their sovereignty. With objective Law it will always be possible that nations may fight because some men believe themselves to be more capable than others of fulfilling the duties of sovereignty. That is not very probable. Individuals wish to increase their landed property because they can lease their new lands. The intensity of their desire would considerably diminish if they found themselves compelled to cultivate and improve with their own labour as much land as they acquired. And, in the final result, would it not be enviable progress if wars broke out, not through disputes over positions of profit but over positions of social service?

Let me repeat that the objective doctrine of Law will not prevail without having first overcome every kind of resistance. The rulers of States, above all, will offer the greatest resistance to any diminution of their power. But the realization of the objective conception in international law is indissolubly linked to its realization in public and private law. The latter implies the constitution of the different social classes in Guilds or Syndicates. This constitution implies, too, the progressive diminution of the power of the governing heads in the States. When the power of rulers has diminished enough, it will not be possible for them to resist successfully the application of the functional principle to international problems. But it will be, above all, the recollection of the horrors of this war, should it succeed in frustrating Germany's aspirations to hegemony, which will tinge with the colour of blood the love of men for absolute sovereignty, and which will make them seek their salvation in a conception of law founded on things.

THE BALANCE OF POWER AS A CONDITION OF CULTURE

IT is not true that this is a war of ideas. It is a war of Powers who are fighting for power. That does not mean that the war does not influence ideas. Every human conflict influences ideas, or at least their realization in social life. Amid the competition of the Stock Exchange the ruin of one financier who happens to be a patron of letters influences literature adversely, while the enrichment of another who loves pictures is favourable to the art of painting ; but the struggles on the Stock Exchange are not on that account struggles between literature and painting, but of money against money in search of more money. The intellectuals who maintain that this is a war of ideas do so because they are thinking of the characteristics of the belligerents instead of thinking of the aims of the war, and because they suppose that if it is not a war of ideas it cannot have any interest for them ; or, at least, it ought not. There are many intellectuals who have not reflected enough on the importance of the factor of power. There are others, on the other hand, who do not believe in any other values than those of power. Against the former we shall argue that it is Utopian to ignore the element of power ; against the latter, that it is blindness to deny the values of the good, the true, and the beautiful. The assertion of ideas and the denial of force is pure mysticism ; the assertion of power and the denial of ideas is pure barbarism.

Even if it were possible to prove that all the belligerents in one group maintained in the same way the primacy of the ideas of liberty and nationality, and that all the Powers in the other group were defending with one mind the primacy of the ideas of authority and Empire, it could not be deduced from that fact that the present war is deciding the conflict between liberty and authority, between nationality and imperialism. If a Liberal and a Conservative go to law, that does not mean that they submit to the verdict of the court the polemic between the ideas of progress and order. It is quite possible that the lawsuit may be concerned only with the ownership of a house. I have seen on a cinematograph a lawyer and a physician boxing. They were not fighting for the primacy of the law or of natural science, but for a woman. Wars have been undertaken for ideological motives, as, for example, the war declared by the European monarchies against the French Convention in 1793. The present war does not propose to achieve the triumph of any idea. It is a war of power. Germany went to war to secure the hegemony of Europe ; the Allies, to prevent her. It is in this way that the war is interpreted by retired soldiers in their club arm-chairs, and these are men, as a rule, of few ideas. That does not mean that their interpretation is false, nor does it lessen the interest with which the war inspires the world. I believe, on the contrary, that it ought to inspire the intellectuals with as much interest as other men. The thesis of this chapter is that European culture is based on the balance of power, and that in fighting for the balance of power England is fulfilling her great historical function of fighting for European culture.

The balance of power, in Europe, has no alternative other than the hegemony of one of its States, as it had no other also in Ancient Greece, whence we derive the two ideas of hegemony and balance. We may lament as much as we like the fact that in this world of power the ideas of the Sermon on the Mount do not prevail ; our lament will be useless. A conflict of power can only be solved in one of two ways : balance or hegemony. In the Middle Ages it was possible to maintain the balance because the Church was opposed to the ambitions of the German Empire ; at the time of the Renaissance the balance was saved because the Reformation undermined the power of the Empire ; in the seventeenth and eighteenth centuries it was England who saved the balance by fighting against the ambitions of France ; in the nineteenth century England remained faithful to her policy of maintaining the balance, but her Government committed the tragic error of not perceiving, until forty years too late, that the Power which threatened the balance was not Russia but Germany.

Now the position is clear. As the Germans crossed the Danube to enter Serbia, the meaning of the war came into the limelight. The Germans do not want to remain in Belgium, but to negotiate with it ; perhaps, too, they do not want to keep Poland, except in so far as to make it an autonomous but tributary kingdom. What they do intend is to expand towards the south-east and to form a great Empire or group of Empires which shall cross the centre of Europe from the north and the Baltic Seas to find its eastern and southern boundaries in the Black Sea, the Persian Gulf, the Red Sea, and the Suez Canal. At one side of this immense stretch of European and Asiatic territory Russia would remain isolated ; at the other side, our side, the Western Powers: France, Italy, England. In the centre of the whole continent, as now in the centre of Europe, the German Empire would remain supreme.

This German Empire would not imply the disappearance of the Austro-Hungarian Empire or the Ottoman Empire, or of the kingdoms of Greece, Bulgaria, and Roumania, provided that they behaved themselves satisfactorily towards the Germans. These empires and kingdoms could remain, as there remain to-day within the German Empire itself the four kingdoms of Prussia, Bavaria, Saxony, and Würtemberg ; the six Grand Duchies of Baden, Hesse, Mecklenburg-Schwerin, Mecklenburg-Strelitz, Saxe-Weimar, and Oldenburg ; five duchies, seven principalities, and the three free cities of Hamburg, Bremen, and Lübeck. The organization of the German Empire is elastic. It is an organization of hegemony by concentric circles. In Prussia the King, with his bureaucracy and territorial aristocracy, is in command. Side by, side with the sovereignty of Prussia the remaining German States maintain their own sovereignty ; but in the affairs of the whole Empire the supremacy of Prussia is assured by the fact that she possesses the majority of votes in the Council of the Empire. Why should not this series of concentric circles be extended? Even at the present time it is a fact that the Prussian General Staff directs the military operations of the whole German Empire ; it also directs those of the Austro-Hungarian and Turkish Armies, and probably the operations of the Bulgarian armies as well.

While the Austro-Hungarian Empire might still exist, it would be possible to attach it more closely to Germany by this system of concentric circles, in such a manner that the German-speaking

Austrians might come to form the first vanguard of the Greater Germany ; the second would be the Hungarians ; the third, the Bohemians; the fourth, the other Slav peoples governed by the Austro-Hungarian Monarchy ; the fifth, the Serbians, in the same state of dependence as the Bosnians and Herzegovinians are in now. Then would come Bulgaria, enlarged at Serbia's expense ; then Greece and Roumania ; and, finally, Turkey, with all the honours of the Ottoman Empire, but governed in the same fashion as Egypt is, with a numerous German and Austrian personnel, who would irrigate the region of Mesopotamia with the waters of the Tigris and the Euphrates in order to provide Northern Germany with raw material from the tropics —coffee, cotton, etc.—and with the foodstuffs which she now has to get from other lands. This new Empire would not need to adopt the title of Empire ; it would not even have to express its real constitution in a written Constitution. It could form itself by a system of commercial treaties, financial monopolies, and military alliances which would render its disruption a matter of great difficulty. The fundamental basis of this Empire would be physical force, consolidated by economic factors. And whenever signs of discontent or disruption made their appearance, the Supreme Government at Berlin would throttle them with a new war of conquest, of which Holland would be the victim one day, Persia the next, Denmark the next, and Egypt the next. The method is simple. Those who were discontented out of idealism would be shot ; those who were discontented out of ambition would be given employment in the newly conquered territories. In this way the new German Rome would gradually extend its boundaries until it comprised the whole of the old continent, Europe

Asia, and Africa, and the rest of the world would be added unto it.

It is against this monstrous dream that the Allies are fighting. I should like to see all the countries now neutral fighting it, too: first, because I believe that its realization is possible, though not probable ; and, secondly, because its realization would be fatal to culture. To which you may reply with the evocation of Imperial Rome. All Imperialistic dreams are no more than remembrances of Ancient Rome. This is because Ancient Rome satisfies one of the perennial longings of the human mind: the longing for grandeur. When I was a child, and my eyes wandered over the engravings that illustrated Mommsen's " History of Rome," I liked to imagine on an enormous scale the eleven forums, the ten great basilicas, the twenty-eight libraries, the nineteen aqueducts, the amphitheatre, the theatres, the temples, and the circuses, rising high above fountains and gardens and sculptures without number. Even now I awake sometimes as I am dreaming of colossal monuments. However civilized a man may be, he always preserves within himself a barbarian fond of fat women, like the Arabs. That lower part of ourselves which prefers quantity to quality, luxury to art, rhetoric to poetry, power to justice, and mass to form will always find its ideal in the Roman Empire. " If you do not know how to build the Parthenon, pile up the Pyramids," was the advice given by Flaubert to a young architect, his nephew.

I was lucky enough not to see Rome until after I had saturated myself, in Florence, with the grace, the life, and the joy of the Middle Ages and the Renaissance. Perhaps that was why the Roman arches and the ruins of the Colosseum and the thermal baths weighed so heavily on me that I

could breathe easily only in the Catacombs.
Mysticism and asceticism are blind alleys. Our
eyes were not made to see the mysteries ; and
self-inflicted torture cannot make us love the good
things more. But in the ruins of Ancient Rome
the mysticism and asceticism of the first Christians
is easy to understand. If the world did not offer
any other values than those of accumulating power
and of expending it in material pleasures, every
refined soul, even if only moderately refined, would
feel inclined to deny the world. Nobody can deny
the utility of the work carried out by Rome in
subduing the peoples on the coasts of the Mediter-
ranean. That work made easier the access of Greek
ideas to the barbarians. Rome was the road over
which Greece passed. But we owe civilization, first,
to Athens and the cities of Hellas ; secondly, to
Florence and the Italian cities ; and, thirdly, to
the European nations. To Rome, the adminis-
trative mind excepted, we owe nothing. The
pomp of Roman literature badly conceals its low
imitative quality. The two central ideas of
her Law, the *imperium* and the *dominium* (State
despotism and private property), are the two great
obstacles which still impede the constitution of
human societies according to the principles of
justice.

It is an historic fact that culture and civilization
arise from nations and cities in the moments in
which, perhaps, they may be aspiring to hegemony,
but in which they do not reach it, since the balance
of power remains with rival countries and towns.
Culture and civilization do not arise from hegemony, but from balance of power. The example
of Germany confirms the rule. The whole of her
culture was produced in that period of uncertainty
and fluidity in which the real hegemony of Austria

had ceased and that of Prussia had not yet come into being. In a previous chapter I have combated the assertion of David Hume in his essay " Of the Rise and Progress of the Arts and Sciences," viz. "*that it is impossible for the arts and sciences to arise, at first, among any people, unless that people enjoy the blessings of a free government*." I attacked this assertion because the word " Liberty " has nowadays, thanks to Mill, the sense of a facultative power, by virtue of which the individual believes himself authorized to defend his country or not to defend it, to serve society or not to serve it, according to his wish. In this sense liberty is anti-social, abominable, and has nothing to do with culture. But one may give to the word " liberty " another meaning, that which it had among the Greeks—the meaning of citizenship or participation in the government ; and in that case David Hume's assertion recovers its full value. ' It is around the problem of the governance of countries, and precisely when the governance of countries constitutes a problem, that civilization has been built up.

The reason of this historic fact is not historical, but philosophical. The central theme of culture is the governance of peoples. It is the central theme because it is the syncretic. For the good governance of peoples a knowledge of the real factors—economics, military power, and arts and crafts—is as necessary as a knowledge of the ideal factors, justice and truth. In the theme of government the facts group themselves in the ideas, and the ideas discipline themselves in the realities. In Plato's Republic we must see, not merely a Utopia, but also a programme to which the Hellenic cities would certainly have tried to adjust themselves if their independence had not been destroyed, first by

Macedonia and then by Rome.   Plato's Republic is not a Utopia, but an anticipation.   But when the cities of Hellas lose their autonomy, Greek thought strays from reality.   Its orators become vagrant jugglers, wandering from city to city, clothing themselves in festive attire to deliver their epideictic speeches of mere show in the market-places, and its philosophers decorate the banquets of the stupid senators of Rome.

Rome, perhaps, would have been a country creative of culture if, at the beginning of her development, she had been contained by neighbouring countries as strong as herself.   Then the struggles between the patricians and the plebeians would have been prolonged indefinitely ; and from these struggles a great political literature would have arisen—not to mention the literature which would have arisen among the Etruscans if they had been able to maintain their independence in the face of Rome.   But Rome was able to subdue her neighbours, and to make herself so powerful that it became possible to satisfy the ambitions of the plebeians at the expense of the conquered countries.   That made the rise of an original culture impossible for Rome.   Men and peoples tend naturally to material expansion.   It is the bestial, eternal, and indestructible side of human nature.   Imperialism is natural to man.   It is, as Seillière says, " the original tendency of human nature to prepare for itself a future of rest and well-being through the rational exercise and increase of its force."   Only when this will to power shatters itself against other wills to power which are opposed and antagonistic to it does the human spirit turn on itself and discover the superior values of the true, the beautiful, and the good.   In this sense the balance of power, both in home and foreign politics, is the condition *sine quâ non* of culture.

To this it may be objected that the balance of power leads to rivalry in armaments, that armaments cost money, and that this money must be withdrawn from social reform, education, culture, etc. To that I simply reply: It is true ; but when a nation devotes the whole of its strength to the ideal of achieving the hegemony, the other nations have no choice but to sacrifice themselves to stop it. But what I do affirm is that the balance of power is not only an essential condition for culture ; it is also essential in order that one day international relations may be based on justice, through the application of the objective principle of law, the Guild or functionarist principle.

The balance of power is as necessary for a good internal policy as for a good external policy. And the reason is this : As soon as a social class acquires absolute superiority over the others, it loses all stimulus to produce objective values. It only cares about maintaining its power or spending it in a life of pleasure, while the other social classes confine themselves either to admiring it or to hating it. When a given class predominates over the others in a society, culture is impossible. Modern nations owe the culture they possess to the rivalry of different governing classes—the territorial capitalists, the shareholding classes, the bureaucracy, the politicians, and even the remains of the ecclesiastic hierarchy. The ideal is not a proletarian régime, but to convert the workmen into ruling classes. For every class tends, naturally, to hegemony. But only when the other classes combined are more powerful than the class or classes nearest to hegemony will they be able to oblige the latter to fulfil their functions, and to be

16

content with the power necessary for these functions. A society of nations strong enough to dominate the most imperious, an organization of social classes capable of acting likewise—that is the balance of power.

THE PRIMACY OF THINGS

THE problem of the primacy of things *versus* the primacy of men is one of the oldest in human culture. It might even be said that the whole of .Western civilization is simply the rotation of the mind round this theme. More than that. What is characteristic of Western civilization is that there have always been in it some men who stood up for the primacy of things. Not that they denied humanity. Only the pessimistic philosophies of the East have tried to deny men, and also things, and to wish for a Nirvana where pain ceases with existence. The partisans of the primacy of things acknowledge the need of men to realize things in this world of ours. The primacy of things means only the doctrine that they form the best criterion for judging men. Protagoras said: " Man is the measure of all things, of those which are as they are, and of those which are not as they are not." The contrary doctrine might be expressed in this other formula: " The things which are, and those which are not but which we wish to be, give us the measure of all men."

A polemic so old—why has it not been settled already? Simply because there is no Supreme Court the jurisdiction of which is acknowledged by both the contending parties. For the upholders of the primacy of things the Supreme Court is truth. They believe that truth is true in itself, that it is a property of some propositions, and not of the men who maintain them, or of the doubt or the certainty with which they maintain them. But the upholders of the primacy of men do not believe in truth. Protagoras held that there were neither true nor false perceptions, but that some were more useful than others. In our own time William James came to the same conclusion when he said that truth is that which gives satisfaction. And the same thing has been said against me: " Those things are true which are perpetually enforced." It could not be otherwise. The doctrine of the primacy of men can be upheld only when truth is denied.

The proposition that "those things are true which are perpetually enforced" tells us that truth is a property which things acquire when they are imposed by force. You add force to a thing, and it becomes true. Truth, therefore, is power. It triumphs because it is power. Christianity is true while it has power; it ceases to be true when it ceases to be powerful. This proposition is coherent so long as it is not cancelled by another proposition which directly contradicts it. But it is a fact that the same people who assert that power has the virtue of transmuting itself into truth believe also in a sort of truth without power, as when they say: " . . . but if truth is so mighty that it must prevail, well, why does it not do so?" Here it is said that truth has no power; whereas before truth is power. Why does not truth prevail? I am not called upon to answer. I have asserted power as a means, and truth as an end; what I have not asserted is the power of truth, or the truth of power. But if I am asked why truth does not prevail in this world of men, I shall say that it does not prevail because many talented men either deny it or do not seek it.

I quite realize that very little is gained when it is shown that a man who does not believe in truth has contradicted himself. A Spanish professor, a pragmatist, used to say: '' They say that I contradict myself ; let them say it ! What is a contradiction? It is to enunciate one idea and then another. Plurality of contradictions implies multiplicity of ideas.'' Pardon, master ! Frequent contradictions only mean that you are wasting your time. But we who believe in truth, or, what amounts to the same thing, we who believe that a proposition cannot be true and not true at the same time feel ourselves morally compelled to offer our apologies when a critic surprises us in the sin of contradiction.

Plato believed that he had refuted Protagoras when he said that the same wind had to be either cold or hot, although some men might think it cold and others hot. Celsius, Réaumur, and Fahrenheit afterwards invented thermometers, which seem to confirm Plato's opinion. If all men withheld their assent from truth, they would not on that account have diminished its value ; they would only have diminished their own value. Nevertheless, Nietzsche called Socrates a decadent, because he discovered objective truth. History says nothing which should lead us to believe that Socrates was physiologically a decadent. It describes him as one of the toughest and boldest soldiers in Athens, capable of out-drinking all his friends, and dying the most beautiful death that ever closed the eyes of man. History will not be able to say as much of Friedrich Nietzsche.

But this point is not pertinent to the argument. Those who believe in the primacy of things may use personal arguments when they are angry, just like those who believe in the primacy of men.

But what the former cannot believe is that personal arguments invalidate a proposition. Nietzsche's theses must be examined by themselves, whether Nietzsche was mad or sane. The proposition that two and two are four is equally, true whether it is traced in the sands or is sculptured in marble, whether it is said by a sane man or a madman, whether it is whispered by the lover into the ear of his beloved, or is uttered by a drunkard strangling his mother in a fit of delirium tremens. And moral and political truths are not less true than the physico-mathematical. The difference is extrinsic to the truth. It consists, in the first place, in the fact that the physico-mathematical truths are useful to us, or at least harmless. But moral and political truths may be fatal to us if our position is based on lies.

Another difference consists in the method of proving truths. We can prove physico-mathematical truths by crucial experiments. Politico-moral truths do not admit of direct proof. Although they are as true as the others, our belief in them cannot be of the same kind, because they are only susceptible of indirect proof, by appeal to Universal History. They are proved by way of examples, and examples are different from experiments in that they cannot be absolutely isolated from the context of social life. But their lesson is clear enough to confirm us in our thesis. For, what is one of the practical results derived from the position which we may adopt with respect to the primacy of things or of men? We who affirm the primacy of things say that positions of social power should not be given to men by virtue of subjective rights, but by virtue of their capacity for the function which they have to fulfil. Those who affirm the primacy of men suppose that there exist subjective rights

of birth from which the social positions of power
are derived, or that there are in some men certain
gifts of Nature which give them the right to command, without the necessity of the jurisdiction in
which their command is exercised being previously
delimited.   Some of these enemies of the study of
things come even to say that: ' " To suggest that
society ' gives ' anything is really absurd.". . . .
" If a man have not the gift of command, for
example, can society give him the power of a com-
mander-in-chief ? "   The reply is in the affirmative.
General Munro was appointed to command the
expeditionary force at the Dardanelles.   Did
he appoint himself ?   You may say that he was
appointed through " evocation of his personal
power."   But the officer who was entrusted with
the landing at Suvla Bay was superseded.   Here
is obviously a case in which society gave power
to a man who did not know how to exercise it.
And the Highest War Lord in Germany was not
nominated through his " gift of command," but
because he happened to be the eldest son of the
Emperor Frederick III.

It is not difficult to discover why the system still
prevails of conferring social power upon certain men
by virtue of purely subjective reasons, such as birth ;
or romantic and subjective reasons, such as the gift
of command, magnetism, etc.   By this method
there is no need to subject men to continual
examinations, as there would be in an " objec-
tivized " society, in which the classes would be
exclusively constituted around things: railways,
mercantile marine, national defence, agriculture,
cattle-raising, industry, education, the post-office,
scientific investigation, art, etc., and in which the
hierarchies: apprentices, journeymen, masters, and
heads of the Guilds, would be formed in accord-

ance with the actual capacities of the men. A system of subjective rights, such as that of giving the leadership of society to the men who possess a pedigree five hundred years old, or the giving of the money of the commonwealth to the sons of successful financiers, saves us from the trouble of examining and re-examining the actual capacities of every man. But if we want the right man in the right place, heredity will help us no more than will the casting of lots.

The doctrine of the primacy of things is easy to understand in theory, though difficult to realize in practice. But, difficult as it is, it is the only one that offers a solution of the conflicts in which we are daily engaged. For example, ought the individual to be sacrificed to the State? Socialism says yes; but that is tyranny. Ought the State to be sacrificed to the individual? Individualism says yes; but that is anarchy. To conciliate this old antagonism between the State and the individual the correlative theory has been invented—the individual is for the State and the State for the individual. But this solution is purely verbal. For the problem arises only when there is a conflict. If there is a conflict, to which does the primacy belong? To say that the individual and the State are correlative is to deny the existence of the conflict, and to seek to cure a cancer by saying that there are no cancers.

Between the defenders of the primacy of the State and the upholders of the primacy of the individual there have recently arisen the upholders of Syndicalism who defend the primacy of societies constituted by the professions. But this does not enable us to find a way out of the conflict; for who shall prevail in case of a conflict between the individual and the syndicate, or between the syndicate and the State or society in general? Here, Syndicalism leaves us in the same perplexity as Socialism. For the question cannot be solved by saying that the Syndicate must have the primacy—which would amount to saying that the Syndicate is always right—the question begins when the Syndicate is wrong, or when the State is wrong, or when the individual is wrong.

And this question is insoluble, absolutely insoluble, so long as we do not clearly realize that every association is an association in one thing, and that this thing must have the primacy in all disputes arising out of the working of the association. There is nothing complicated in this thought. It is so simple that, once understood, it imposes itself on the mind with the force of a category. But it is new. It is strangely new. All theories of association—from which theories of the State are derived—may be classified in two groups—the authoritarian theories, which see the essence of associations in the fact that within them there are some individuals who command and others who obey ; and the democratic theories, for which the enduring essence of associations lies in the associated. Even Duguit, in spite of his calling his doctrine " The theory of objective right," does not look beyond human solidarity in his search for the basis of associations. According to Duguit, men associate because they are solidary, because they have mutual need of one another. Duguit does not see that the profound secret of associations consists, not in the fact that men have mutual need of one another, but in the fact that they need the same thing. Objective right cannot arise from the fact that men have mutual need of one another. This fact can only originate rights of a trans-individual kind, not objective. The secret of associations lies

in the fact that men need the same thing—whether
this thing be a game, as in football associations ;
or a territory, as in States ; or a religious dogma,
as in the Churches.

Human solidarity can only exist in things. We
do not associate directly with another person ; it
is friendship or love or community of interests or
ideas that makes us associate with him. The individuality of the other person always remains for us
the unknowable mystery and the unpierceable wall.
Without the mediation of the thing association is
impossible.

The other person does not and cannot enter into
a direct relation of rights and duties with us through
the mere fact that he is another person. Rights do
not arise from personality. This idea is mystic and
unnecessary. Rights arise primarily from the relation of the associated with the thing that associates
them, as circumference arises from the relation of
its points with the centre. It is clear that, apart
from the relation of the associated with the thing
that associates them, there are in an association
all kinds of relations among the associated. The
reason is that all men belong at the same time to
a plurality of associations. We are all partners,
whether we like it or not, in our planet earth, and
we are all residents in some borough and citizens
of some State—from which it is to be deduced that
no association can claim absolute jurisdiction over
us. Hence, jurisdictional conflicts are inevitable.
What I say is that the reason why many of these
conflicts are unnecessarily multiplied and aggravated
is that Law has not been based on the relation of
the associated with the thing that associates them ;
but has been sought to be founded directly on the
associated themselves, independently of the thing
associating them. Thus one speaks of the rights

of the sovereign, or of the rights of man, as if they were inherent to the condition of sovereign or man. Against this tradition I deny that rights are inherent, and I affirm that all rights are adherent. They arise, mathematically speaking, purely in function of the thing. No function, no rights.

The Christian Church may offer to all Westerners the model of associations. It is an association founded on the central dogmas of original sin and the Redeemer who guarantees the possibility of grace. The isolated individual, powerless to preserve his faith and to adjust his life to his dogma, associates in the Church. The Church is an association founded on a thing, Christianity. The Church, or assembly of the faithful, is, therefore, an instrument and not an end. In no association, nor in the whole of the associations, can the associated form more than an instrument, never an end. Formerly, I used to like the distinction made by Rousseau between the " general will " and the " will of all." Rousseau believed that the " general will " could not err. This amounted to considering the general will as an end and not as a means. In that Rousseau was wrong. The end of an association is not the association, but those things which the association proposes to itself. The end of the Church consists in maintaining and propagating Christianity. It may be said that we men are organs of the associations, and that the associations are organs of men. Both are organs, instruments, means ; what is not an organ is the end of the association. The relation between the organ and the end is the function. And the external regulation of this relation is the Law.

When the history of the Church is studied, it is perceived that her conflicts are of two kinds :

superior conflicts, in which the faithful quarrel over
dogmas ; and inferior conflicts, in which the
ecclesiastics quarrel over jurisdiction. In the last
few centuries the ecclesiastics have hardly quarrelled
over anything but jurisdiction ; questions of dogma
left them cold. To be a Catholic is to consider
as the supreme authority the Pope of Rome ; to
be Orthodox is to believe in the highest rank of
the Four Patriarchs ; to be an Episcopalian, Presby-
terian, or Congregationalist is to believe in the
primacy of the bishops, the presbyters, and the
congregation. In this miserable dispute over power
Christianity has been left to perish. To such an
extent has the Church forgotten to renew its reasons
and to vivify the experiences on which its dogmas
and hopes are founded that now it is possible, even
for men reputed to be intelligent, to ignore
Christianity—and with Christianity the only satisfactory explanation of the human tragedy.

What is essential in an association is the end it
proposes to itself. The association and the associated
are nothing but the instruments for this end. The
problem of authority is only instrumental for the
instrument that the association forms. Questions
of authority are of the third order. Those of the
first order refer to the end ; those of the second,
to the law of the association ; those of the third,
to the jurisdiction of authorities. Who is the
authority in case of a conflict? In the reply one
has to distinguish two questions : that of fact and
that of right. The authority of fact is that which
possesses the power to impose itself within the
association ; the authority of right is that which
best serves the end of the association. How, then,
solve jurisdictional conflicts according to right? By
seeing that social power is conferred according to
the functions of the associated, and the functions

according to capacities. And how is this to be achieved? It is to be achieved as far as possible by never losing sight of the end of the association. The standard which ought to serve us to settle questions of authority and power is the end of the association. The triumph of this standard is what I call the primacy of things.

Men have quarrelled, are quarrelling, and will quarrel over power. The reason is that the essence of man is power also, and one of the sides of power is the tendency to grow at the expense of others. Man is tending to power not only through his animal condition of natural force, but because he receives from his human nature the tendency to pride, which is an aspect of his original sin. But man considered purely as power has no rights ; for into the concept of right there enters a positive ethical factor. Rights only arise when man enters into relation with the good, either to preserve the existing goods or to create new ones. In function of the good, in the relation between man and good, rights arise. Every right is functional. Every right which is not functional, all subjective rights, all the so-called rights of man, all the rights of sovereigns, are not rights in reality ; they are simply powers.

The German theory proclaims the primacy of the State over the nation, that is to say, of the ruler over the ruled. The liberal democratic theory proclaims the primacy of the nation over the State, that is to say, of the ruled over the ruler. Both theories are based on a distinction between the individual and the super-individual values. The theory of the primacy of things does not deny this distinction. The association is one thing and the associated another. But what it does deny is that the super-individual values—it would be better to call them trans-individual values—are intrinsically of a superior category to the individual values. Both values are purely instrumental. The association—and with it all the institutions (family, property, State, Church, Guild, etc.)—is purely an instrument, like man. If in the association there are final values, they are its ends. And these ends are divided into good and evil ; because men associate for evil also.

When values are divided, not into positive and negative—good and evil—but into superior and inferior, the classification has to be made according to their final or instrumental character. Final and superior values are the goods in themselves—such as moral satisfaction, scientific discovery, or artistic creation. Instrumental and inferior values are those which have no intrinsic value, but are only tools for the production of final values. To this class of values belong man and all his institutions and associations. Within the instrumental values one has to distinguish a category inferior even to man himself. To this inferior category belong all economic values. Economics and all its values are as instrumental to man as man and all his institutions and associations ought to be to the good, the true, and the beautiful.

The concept of value was invented by economics, and from economics has ascended to philosophy. It may be said that nowadays there is no other philosophy than that of the values. Economics, on the other hand, has died as an autonomous science, to become a side of history—that side of history that endeavours to explain the relations of the instrument man with his instruments of production, distribution, and consumption. This mental revolution has been carried out in the last twenty years. But few are the people who know it to be an accomplished fact, and still fewer those who realize its significance.

The doctrine of the primacy of things does not assume that all conflicts can be avoided. The only thing it positively offers to us is a standard for settling them justly. In suppressing subjective rights it tells us that only he who best serves the common good has the right to come first. But its educative utility is not inferior to that which it offers us as a standard of justice. In telling us that our value is purely instrumental, it teaches us to smile at our pretensions. In spite of it men will go on trying to impose themselves on one another. But it may become the true foundation of democracies. Up to now it has been sought to found democracy on the principle that every man is a sovereign owing obedience to no one. This principle forgets that a king wants a kingdom; and it is of no use our declaring ourselves sovereigns if we lack subjects to command. To call us kings and to deny us kingdoms is to turn us into pretenders perpetually conspiring. Democracy can be real only if we decide to serve the common good, either spontaneously or through mutual coercion. The true foundation of democracy is the conviction that no man—emperor, pope, or workman—is entitled to any consideration other than that due to a possible instrument of the eternal values. Instruments are used when they are in good order ; repaired when damaged, and thrown away when useless.

DEATH AND RESURRECTION

HOW can men be cured of the excessive value which they grant to their personality? The reactionaries and obscurantists say that by suppressing popular education the number of men who possess self-consciousness will disappear or diminish, and it will, therefore, be possible to make them live a life of obedience and faith. Perhaps the reactionaries are right ; but it is also possible to cure with more culture the evil increased by culture. Why should it not be possible to sharpen our culture up to such a point that we may come to see ourselves with the same eyes as we see the others? When we judge the others we do not grant to them the same value as they grant to themselves. We know quite well that the proudest of men may lack any value. The positive value of a man is measured by what he produces, and his negative value by what he consumes ; and there is no other objective measure of value. It won't do for me to believe myself to be the first of men. If what I produce is worth less than what I consume, my value is negative ; by which I mean that the world would gain if I ceased to exist. But in this sacrifice of personality to objective values there remains an element of irrationality which we shall not be able to understand unless we realize at the same time the nature of heroism.

A few months ago the newspapers spoke of a

French artillery officer who, mortally wounded on the battlefield, began to talk to his companion about the supreme beauty of dying for one's country, and who, when feeling the shadows of death upon his eyes, cried : " Vive la France ! " and expired. I cannot tell what image of France crossed the mind of the dying man—perhaps the ascendant France of Joan of Arc and Rheims ; perhaps the noon of France under Louis XIV. and Napoleon ; perhaps the sanguinary spectre of the French Departments devastated by the invader ; perhaps the ironical recollection of a bourgeois, rationalist, and pacific France, satisfied with the Here and Now, but far away from that region of sacrifice, creation, and destruction which seems to be the central point of life. What is probable is that the officer died in the intuitive certainty that his life had not been lived in vain. He probably believed that his blood, in one form or another, would not be fruitless : either because the death of her sons immediately assures the continuity of France, or that the same spirit which to-day leads French soldiers to die for their country will to-morrow, perhaps, induce the women of the land to sacrifice their momentary selfishness on the altars of the survival of the Gallic blood. What is certain is that through the soul of this dying officer and of many other thousands of French heroes passed in the last moments the Themes of Death and Resurrection which, in their intermingling, form the fundamental mystery of nearly every religion.

One of the best modern English books I have read, " Themis : A Study of the Social Origins of Greek Religion," by Miss Jane Harrison, satisfactorily proves the thesis that the Olympic gods, with their athanasia or " eternity through not dying," achieved at the cost of life, were elaborated

17

by the Hellenic spirit centuries after Dionysos and the other gods of Death and Resurrection — the symbols of the succession of the seasons of the year, of the permanence of the tribe amid the deaths of individuals, and of the universal palingenesis of Nature. From Miss Harrison's book we see that the gods of classic Greece gradually get rid of everything that, in primitive times, identified them with the cyclic pulsations of life ; they expel from Olympus all the gods or daimons who still retain the feet of a goat or the body of a cow or serpent as if to indicate their earthly origin ; and they end by turning themselves into mere negations of the " mystery-gods " of fertility.

" So far then," writes Miss Harrison, " our conception of the Olympian is mainly negative. He refuses the functions of the totemistic daimon, he sheds his animal or plant form. He will not be a daimon of Earth, nor yet even of the Sky ; above all he refuses to be a year-daimon with his function of ceaseless toil. He will not die to rise again, but chooses instead a barren immorality. He withdraws himself from man and lives remote, a ' jealous god.' " " The Olympian has clear form, he is the ' principium individuationis ' incarnate ; he can be thought, hence his calm, his *sophrosyne*. The mystery-god is the life of the whole of things, he can only be felt—as soon as he is thought and individualized he passes, as Dionysos has to pass, into the thin, rare ether of the Olympian. The Olympians are of conscious thinking, divided, distinct, departmental ; the mystery-god is the impulse of life through all things, perennial, indivisible."

What Miss Harrison has done with paganism can also be done, and with less labour, with the religion of Israel. Although it may be truly said that the religion of Israel and of the Old Testament is the only one that was never acquainted with mysteries or mythologies, a reading of the prophets is enough to convince one that among the Jews, too, the concept of God underwent an evolution analogous to that which, among the Greeks, changed Dionysos into Apollo. The God of Moses still remembers that other divinity which primitive Israel worshipped in the symbol of the Golden Calf. He was still an immanent, national, actual God who spoke directly through the mouth of the prophets. And the later prophets devoted themselves to little more than ridding the idea of God of those natural-istic traits which recalled, as did the Golden Calf, the periodical Death and Resurrection of Nature. The God of Israel was gradually outgrowing the confines of Israel and of the Earth until he made himself completely transcendental, unknowable, and unimaginable—a mere concept of righteousness and justice, even by the time of the Prophet Amos.

It is curious to note that this progressive ration-alizing of the idea of God is always effected at the cost of Death and Resurrection. It is signifi-cant enough that the God of the Decalogue—who was still the God of Israel and not yet of the world—should have forgotten to include in his Commandments that of giving one's life for one's country in the hour of danger, and of perpetuating life in successive generations. The first prophet to speak of God as a God of Love was Hosea. Unhappy in his marriage with a frivolous woman, Hosea conceived the ambition of fanning her sparks of goodness into a pure flame. In this relation of the loving husband to the beloved, whom he wishes to save not only by tenderness, but also by discipline, Hosea saw a symbol of the relationship existing between the Creator and His creatures. It might be thought that this amorous conception of the deity would have made Hosea more indulgent to the rites which recalled the old gods of fertility. Not at all. No one mocked more bitterly the symbols of the Golden Calf ; no one more strictly separated the cult of Nature from' the cult of Divinity. Although the naturalistic rites had millennial traditions, Hosea saw in them only a corrupt and corrupting paganism of which Israel had to cleanse herself.

Even to-day it is characteristic of the upholders of a purely rationalist morality to dislike any standard of conduct which is based on the mystery of Death and Resurrection. It might be said that the morality which such people preach is purely spatial, in the sense that they wish to extend justice to all men and nations over the entire surface of the earth. This spatial morality, which is that of the cardinal virtues, may be called rationalistic, that is, selfish, because its results are immediately and pleasantly apparent, in the sense that if we behave with prudence, justice, fortitude, and temperance towards our fellow-men we thereby extend spatially the action of the moral sense, and thus free ourselves from the fear that our misconduct might make us the victims of revenge. But Mr. Benjamin Kidd has already told us that this spatial ethic is not enough. Mr. Kidd could not see the possibility of the permanence of a civilization unless by rooting it in an act of faith. Without the sacrifice of the present generation for the sake of the generations to come, humanity would die out even though it had succeeded in making social justice prevail in every corner of the globe. And this sacrifice of the visible to the invisible, of the present to the future, cannot be consciously achieved by the practice of the cardinal or rational virtues. It requires, in addition, the aid of the theological : Faith, the root ; Hope, the flower ; and Charity, the fruit.

When humanity is located in space, it is only logical that the ethical ideal should lead us to wish that the earth might be changed into an Olympus without cradles or graves inhabited by immortal gods. As this is impossible, many " spatial " moralists recommend the ideal of reducing, as far as possible, the number of births and deaths. Thus we may explain the pacifist and Malthusian ideas which have become so widespread in our days. The blind alley into which these ideas lead us was most candidly revealed by Mr. William Archer in an article in the *Daily News*, in which he affirmed the antithesis of " Fecundity, versus Civilization " ; for, if fecundity is the contrary of civilization, the civilization to which Mr. Archer aspires must be sterility.

In the struggle between societies or sections of society, heroic and religious, with societies so rationalistic and calculating that their members cannot decide either to defend them with arms or perpetuate them by maternity, there is no doubt that the latter must succumb. Some rationalists try to meet this danger by proposing measures which may induce calculating societies to perpetuate themselves. Mr. Bertrand Russell has recently devoted a lecture to this question. It is obvious that the intervention of society in these problems is just, because it is not right that good women should suffer the burdens and risks of maternity while the selfish women enjoy the privileges which their voluntary sterility grants them. That is why I am favourable to compulsory maternity, which naturally implies maternity grants. But this measure of justice does not relieve us of the need of a heroic morality. A State or a Guild of a thousand members which pays every year the cost of forty new children will have to sacrifice itself much more than another which only pays for ten more children every year. What happens here is that we have transferred to the corporation the cost that now falls upon the individual. This measure will be just because in consequence of it the bad individuals will also pay for the raising of future generations, while at present only the good do so. But the need of heroism and faith will always be the same.

Compared with this sterility of the "rationalizing reason," there is a spring breeze in the impulse which leads Miss Harrison to follow M. Bergson in his desire "to apprehend life as one, as indivisible, yet as perennial movement and change," and nevertheless to disown the dogmas and even the symbols through which the full life of Dionysos transforms itself into the empty abstraction of Apollo. If I had to choose between Mr. Archer and Miss Harrison, I should remain, naturally, with Miss Harrison. Between an absolute, teleological, iron monism, such as that of the religion of Israel, and an absolute meaningless and fluent pluralism, such as that of Dionysos and Cybele ; between a sterile civilization and a fecundity without sense, I should rather give up the meaning than life ; I would sacrifice the Commandments of Jehovah rather than those of Nature. For I may or may not be a man who lives conformably to the Law ; but I cannot do otherwise than live conformably to Nature.

But I am not bound to choose. Every religion which has lasted in the world has necessarily had to be a mixture of the vital principle and of the rational principle ; because the world, with all its creatures, is of precisely such a mixture. It was not for nothing that in the Temple of the Oracle at Delphi the year was divided into the rites sacred to Dionysos and those sacred to Apollo ; for although it is impossible to think simultaneously of an immortal and of a god that dies and rises again, yet when our spirit passes from the world in space to the world in time, it finds that it can establish a profound affinity between its two pagan symbols, and can see in Apollo the projection of Dionysos in space, and in Dionysos the projection of Apollo into time—in Apollo a Dionysos visualized in plastic, and in Dionysos an Appollo fluent in music.

Thus, too, our Christianity. For " we preach Christ crucified, unto the Jews a stumbling-block, and unto the Greeks foolishness " (1 Cor. i. 23) ; the Jews and rationalists call us pagans and tell us that our God dies and rises again, like Dionysos. And why are we not to be called heathens? Heathens we are ; heathens and Jews, both. By the side of the transcendent god who cannot be represented or thought, such as Jehovah or the Immovable Mover of Aristotle, we place a god who dies and rises again, and this god permits us to exclaim triumphantly, with St. Paul : " O death, where is thy sting? O grave, where is thy victory? " (1 Cor. xv. 55), and then we declare that there is only one god, and not two. We think of God as transcendent and immovable, or as immanent and vital, and then we say that His distinct and separate Persons form no more than one God. We admit that we cannot explain this mystery of the Trinity ; but we add for the sceptical reader that this mystery of the divinity is no more mysterious than that of the first reality which presents itself to his eyes.

For it is characteristic of every reality, as, for

instance, the piece of paper I am writing on, that everything in it flows and does not advance by leaps ; that it is continuous and yet changes incessantly ; and that in the whole of Nature no particular change is exactly like another, but only more or less analogous. Everything is continuous and everything changes. These are the two principles of reality : it is continuous, because we cannot conceive of a reality which could be discontinuous ; it is heterogeneous, because it is continually changing itself into something else, and change presupposes heterogeneity. And this unity of continuity and heterogeneity—a necessary postulate—is that which gives to reality its character of irrationality. As, in the smallest of its parts, reality is a continuous heterogeneity, its unity slips fatally away from our concepts. And not only vital reality, as M. Bergson says, but all reality, including the so-called inert matter.

Every reality is a continuous heterogeneity—heterogeneity is change ; change, death; continuity, resurrection ; every reality is something that survives, dies, and rises again, something of whose continuity and heterogeneity we cannot think at the same time, but in which we must suppose that there exists a unity of continuity and heterogeneity that is not rational. We cannot make reality rational except by artificially suppressing its heterogeneity, as in mathematics and physical science ; or by suppressing its continuity and cutting it up arbitrarily into segments, as we do in history or the descriptive sciences. But the enthusiastic Bergsonism of Miss Harrison carries her too far when it leads her to see a danger, "an almost necessary disaster," in "each and every creed and dogma." Are we to suppress in ourselves the tendency which leads us to theorize on our experiences, and, as this theorizing on our experiences is the basis of personality, are we also to suppress personality?

The fact that consciousness of personality is dangerous for societies, in so far as it isolates individuals, has induced some young Frenchmen to invent the " unanimist " ideal. Miss Harrison has published an apologia of " unanimisme " in England. Its credo consists in submerging the individual consciousness in the " blood " of the association or collectivity. But individual consciousness is, if not as an end, as an instrument, one of the highest values. It is not possible to suppress it without making all human culture disappear with it. To wish to suppress it is to wish to go back to savagery. What is good and positive in " unanimisme " is the acknowledgment that reason is not enough to make us heroic, and that heroism is necessary to maintain civilized societies. In societies that have lost the joy of battle for the sake of battle, and have learnt to enjoy love while being afraid of the burdens of the family, the supreme functions of maternity and of the defence of the country must be based on heroism. We are no longer sufficiently primitive, as Miss Harrison would like us to be, to trust to the instinct of the species ; and reason will never find arguments convincing enough to persuade a soldier that he ought to die in a trench, or a selfish woman that she ought to bear a child. When we deal with these things reason must bow. Their perplexities can only be solved by heroism, and heroism must be founded on faith. In heroism, practical faith, and in faith, theoretical heroism, we find a unity superior to instinct and to reason, and which includes both in a mixture analogous to that of continuity and heterogeneity which constitutes every reality.

If we cannot conceive reality but as a continuous heterogeneity, how can we conceive of the God of this Reality but both as continuous or eternal and as heterogeneous or changing, that is, dying and rising again? What has Miss Harrison in her book but a dogma of Dionysos? What has Bergson in his "Evolution Créatrice" but a dogma of life? And why disaster in dogmas when dogmas, too, are heterogeneous continuities which die and rise again? No reader, on reading this chapter for the second time, will read in it what he read there for the first. Some of his ideas will have died, but others will have risen from the corruption of the letter. In all propositions and dogmas there is an element of truth or falsity, unalterable, eternal, and independent of our will and of life. But the knowledge and interpretation of propositions and dogmas die and rise again. Eternity and mutability fuse together in propositions as in realities. The psychological moment is always death and resurrection. Eternity is extra-psychological.

And thus this war, a magnifying-glass, makes us live again, in the faith of a French artillery officer, the profound life of the dogma of Death and Resurrection. In times of peace we had almost forgotten that life is essentially a tragedy: the tragedy of Death and Resurrection. We had fallen into the ridiculous aspiration towards an athanasia far from the flux of life. The example of the heroes who die that their country may live will stimulate the nations to give up their dream of a Malthusian and pacifist Olympus; and thinkers to adjust, as far as possible, their theories to the mystery of life and reality: Death and Resurrection.

.   .   .   .   .

To sum up what I have written: The principle of function is a better base of societies than the principles of authority and liberty. It is better because

it is more just.   And when I say that it is more just
I assert in the principle of function a quality independent of the wills of men.   It is more just whether
they like it or not.   But in order to triumph it is
necessary that men should like it—all men ; or at
any rate the most powerful and influential.   How
can they be made to like it ?   The way will be prepared by the historians who study the present war.
I myself have no doubt that its horrors must be
attributed to the fact that the world has fallen a
prey to the two antagonistic and incompatible principles of authority and liberty.   The war will have
shown that the more unjust of these two principles
—although the more efficient—is that of unlimited
authority.   It is the more unjust because no man
has a subjective right to command others.   It is the
more efficient, provided that the authorities are not
stupid, because it unifies the social forces in the
direction prescribed by the authority, and because
it implies a principle of order.   The mere fact that
a combination of half the world was necessary to
defeat Germany is proof of its efficiency.   The
strength of the liberal principle lies in its respect
for vocation.   But in the liberal principle there is
no efficiency, for there is no unity of direction.
Nor is there justice in it, for it allows some individuals to invade the field of others.   The idea of
liberty leads men to act as if every letter printed in
this article expanded right and left and tried to
conquer the space occupied by the adjoining letters.
The result of absolute liberty is universal confusion.
But the reason why both these principles of
authority and liberty should be rejected is the
same for each :   that both principles are founded
on subjective rights.   And these rights are false.
Nobody has a subjective right to anything ; neither
rulers nor ruled.

This conclusion will be reached by historians and thinkers. But that is not enough. It is not enough for men to know that it is necessary to sacrifice all kinds of rights founded on personality in order to establish society on a firm basis of justice. Personality must be sacrificed. That is not only a theory but action. The critique may refute authority and liberty as bases of society. But to the conviction that our true life consists in being functionaries of absolute values we arrive only by an act of faith, in which we deny that our ego is the centre of the world, and we make of it a servant of the good. This act of faith is a kind of suicide, but it is a death followed immediately by resurrection. What we lose as personalities we reconquer, multiplied, as functionaries. The man who asks for money simply for himself cannot ask for it with the same moral confidence as he who asks for it in order to study a problem or to create social wealth. St. Paul says (i Cor. xv. 44) that in death " It is sown a natural body," but that in the resurrection " It is raised a spiritual body." The doctrine of Death and Resurrection opens also the way for the submission of man to higher things.

FUNCTIONS AND VALUES

THE objective doctrine of Law is not bound to any particular table of values. It only requires for its basis some table of values ; and every human society has one or another. A society may believe, like Bentham, that the supreme value is pleasure ; or, like Ostwald, energy ; or like " something in the City," wealth ; or, like Ruskin, that " there is no wealth but life " ; or, like the classical moralists, that the supreme values are the good, the true, and the beautiful ; and that man and human institutions and economic values are only instruments for the absolute values. Given any scale of values, those men or associations of men are functionaries who devote themselves to maintaining or increasing values. To those functionaries are due the powers, rights, dignities, and pay corresponding to their function. The men or associations of men who do not devote themselves to preserving or increasing values are not functionaries ; and, therefore, they ought not to have any rights at all. And those who destroy existing values are criminals who deserve punishment. The principle of objective right simply says that rights ought only to be granted to men or associations of men in virtue of the function they fulfil, and not on any pretences of a subjective character.

It is for the Legislature to determine the hierarchy, character, numbers, powers, and pay of the different functions. It is for the examining courts to designate the individuals who may be judged fit for the fulfilment of the different functions. The wisest thing would be that shoemakers should designate shoemakers. In this the functional system would fit without violence into the traditional framework of human society. Even to-day it is lawyers who examine budding lawyers; and it is soldiers who pass or reject candidates for the army. But that is done only in some professions. The son of the rich man, for example, need not undergo any examination previously to being admitted into one of the most coveted of social positions. He is admitted into the Guild of the Idle Rich simply because he is the son of his father. But as the functional system does not recognize subjective rights, it would not permit vast sums of money to be handled by a man unless he had previously demonstrated his financial competence; and the bankers in a functional society will work for fixed pay, like those post-office employees who at present carry out several banking functions.

In order that the functional principle may triumph in the world it is not necessary for men to assemble in a Universal Parliament and say: "Up to now we have based laws on the subjective principles of authority and liberty. Henceforth, we shall base them on the principle of function." What matters it that the functional idea shall gradually make a way for itself among the leaders of public opinion: political men, professors, and publicists. To attain this end, two things only need to be proved: (1) that it is just, and (2) that it is expedient.

Its justice scarcely needs defence. Objective rights alone can be consciously just. Subjective right may be just only by chance. Every subjective right, whether individual or collective, is intrinsically

antagonistic to the very idea of justice. There is no man who can have a just right to be an emperor unless he possesses the aptitudes necesary for fulfilling the functions of an emperor ; nor is there a nation which has the right to constitute itself a sovereign State if it lacks the indispensable conditions for exercising the function of sovereignty. At bottom every subjective right is analogous to that which the owner of land possesses of depriving his neighbour of air and light. The whole horror of modern capitalism may be deduced from the famous Art. xvii of the " Declaration of the Rights of Man " : " As property is an inviolable and sacred right, nobody can be deprived of it, if it is not clearly required by public necessity, legally acknowledged, and on condition of a just and previous compensation." The juridical conception of the French Revolution was pre-eminently subjective ; but no less so is that which grants to a man, solely because he is the head of the Romanoff family, autocratic power over all the Russias. According to the functional principle, no man or association of men shall be able to say that anything belongs to him by a subjective title. Nobody has a subjective right to anything. No rights or powers ought to be granted to men or associations of men other than those necessary for the fulfilment of the functions entrusted to them. Power and right are conditioned by the function. To adjust power to function is obviously just.

What must be defended is the expediency or practicability of the functional principle. This defence will be easier if we make clear the failure of subjective rights. That is not difficult. Subjective rights fail because they are, in their very essence, unlimited. If, for instance, you proclaim the absolute right of a sovereign to a territory, with this right you have proclaimed the right of this sovereign to all the territories of the earth ; for every territory has frontiers which are a menace to his sovereignty. The Germans have told us that they require Metz to secure their Rhine Provinces ; to secure Metz they have tried to make themselves masters of Verdun ; if they were in possession of Verdun they would want Chalons ; if they were in possession of Chalons they would want Paris ; and latterly they have seriously complained that the English blockade may endanger their territorial conquests. But if you proclaim the rights of man to property, liberty, etc., the inevitable result will be the hell of free competition and the exploitation of man by man. And if you try to remedy the evils arising from free competition by proclaiming the right of the workmen to a minimum wage, in order to make this right effective you will have to close your frontiers to the workmen of poorer or more fecund countries ; and the final result will be the war of races. And that is because all juridical systems founded on subjective principles tend to legitimize an unbridled ambition which impels men to destroy one another—and not for just causes, but simply for lust of power.

The reason why subjective rights have been able to prevail up to now is that the Renaissance preached the free development of human personality when America and the route to the Eastern Indies had been discovered. The men who lived between the year 1500 and the past generation must have thought of the world as if it were of inexhaustible dimensions. A conception of right as unlimited privilege—that is to say, a conception in which there is no limit to the amount of power which every man or association of men may appropriate—can be practicable only in an infinite world ; for it matters

little if some men or associations of men take possession of greater quantities of land than they, can cultivate when the total amount of the disposable land is practically unlimited. In circumstances that we call normal, we do not care if men consume more food than they really need. But when provisions become scarce in a beleaguered fortress they are put on rations.

But the world has now been explored. There are now titles of property or sovereignty to the whole cultivable extension of the planet. It is not by mere accident that the same generation which has discovered the two poles of the earth and has explored the ultimate corners of the world should have to witness the horrors of a universal war. If in the name of the right of first occupier some States have taken possession of vacant territories, the Germans, late arrivals at the distribution of the world, are endeavouring now to cancel the existing right in the name of force—another right equally subjective. But no subjective principle can undo the injustice in the distribution of wealth created by other subjective principles. The force of the Allies will be opposed to that of the Germans. Rights founded on liberty will rise against those founded on authority. To-morrow the subjective rights of the coloured races will be opposed to the subjective rights of the white races of to-day. So long as these subjective rights are not limited, there can be no remedy for the injustices arising from the fact that some nations and individuals possess everything, or almost everything, and other nations and individuals possess nothing, or hardly anything. And, as it is not possible to perpetuate either this injustice or the state of war derived from it, the result will be that men will be bound to seek some way of limiting subjective rights, by the creation

18

of a normative right, a right of rights, or a right
to right, which can be based only on the principles
of function.

In this need to limit the subjective rights of men
and of human associations the functional principle
will find its main practical support. It is the very
logic of things, as much as the logic of its theory,
which will make it triumph. Humanity cannot
acknowledge in perpetuity and unconditionally either
the rights of Rockfeller to his millions, or those
of the Brazilian Government to absolute sovereignty
over the immense unexploited wealth of the Amazon
Valley, or those of the Kaiser to set the world on
fire. In order that the vast mass of men may
enjoy security and sufficiency in a limited world,
all subjective rights must be made subordinate to
a right of a superior origin.

.   .   .   . |.

With that we have said that it is not necessary
to maintain a definite table of values to uphold
the functional doctrine. But as I have supported
a fixed hierarchy of values, let me briefly explain
it, although with the full knowledge that the theme
is in truth inexhaustible. (1) The final or supreme
values are, in my judgment, moral satisfaction,
scientific discovery, and artistic creation. (2) The
instrumental value, par excellence, is man and his
associations and institutions. (3) The instrumental
values for the instrument man are those which may
be called by the name of economic values : power,
wealth, pleasure, etc. In fixing this scale I must
first meet the objection of those who identify the
moral value, which belongs to the first category,
with the value man, which belongs to the second.
To my mind, moral satisfaction does not consist in
man doing what he wants, or what other men want

him to do, but in the submission of man to some abstract moral values such as veracity, humility, fortitude, fidelity, justice, pity, etc., some of which may be benefical to men and others prejudicial, according to the circumstances of time and place.

The reason why it is impossible for me to accept any other scale of values, or to change the order of this scale, is not difficult to explain. It is thought out in such a way that the first category of values includes the second and third ; the second includes the third but not the first ; and the third does not include either the first or second. It is not possible for men to realize morality, science, and beauty if there are no men, and if men do not possess such economic values as are necessary for their subsistence. On the other hand, there may be men who do not care for the good, the true, and the beautiful. We all know cases of men or human societies who could if they wished, or if they were forced, devote themselves to increasing or preserving the amount of goodness or truth or beauty there is in the world ; but who devote themselves exclusively to augmenting their power or their wealth or their pleasures. And experience of the factory system during the nineteenth century has proved that some human societies may devote themselves to increasing wealth at the expense of the lives of their members.

If our tale of values is accurate, the evil results from its alteration. Why is capitalism bad? Because it places the economic value, which belongs to the third category, above the second, which is the value man. But let us suppose the case of a democratic society which deliberately refused to lend its help to the service of the good for the good's sake, of science for science sake, or of beauty for beauty's sake. I have been told that the workmen who study at the Universities of Oxford and Cambridge do not object to the staffs of professors and lecturers being well paid; but they resent the fact that individual fellows are paid by the colleges to carry on such investigations as they like without being called upon to lecture. If this criterion prevailed, we should sacrifice the value of science, which is a supreme value, to the value man, which is merely instrumental.

This scale of values does not pretend to solve all the conflicts that may arise. Man is fallible, and again and again he may consider as a supreme value that which is merely an instrumental value. If the present dominant doctrine of subjective rights demands that there shall be in the world a hundred parliaments, with twenty or thirty thousand legislators devoted incessantly to readjusting subjective rights to social necessities, to the spirit of justice and to the ambitions of men, no one has a right to expect that a simple scale of values can solve problems for which not even the Decalogue has been able to provide a solution.

But in the last few months there has arisen—and has been solved—a conflict about values which will remain in the history of humanity as a classical example. The German Government has held that, as the knowledge of the possibilities of submarines came after the international laws regulating naval warfare, submarines shall be free to torpedo any ship at sight, merchantman or war vessel. The American Government replied to this contention by saying that, as the passengers and crews of merchant vessels are entitled to safety, it is for the submarine to adjust itself to international law, and not for international law to adjust itself to the submarine. The American Government has won its case; and our scale of values says that this victory is just because in it the instrumental value of that human society which we call Germany, has been sacrificed to that supreme value of pity as codified in the international conventions.

But I repeat that the fundamental reason of my scale is that when it proclaims as supreme values the good, the true, and the beautiful it does include and protect man and his economic values, although it may limit in man the free expansion of what is bad in human nature—lust and pride.

THE FUNCTIONAL PRINCIPLE

THERE are, in short, four reasons which give us cause to hope that the men of to-morrow will decide to found their societies and their laws on the principle of function.

The first lies in the necessity to find a higher principle which may serve as a remedy against the excesses of authority. In a sense, we are faced here with an insoluble problem. The old question of constitutional law, Quis custodiet ipsos custodes? has never found and will never find a satisfactory answer. There is no other guardianship for the guardians than the moral sense of the other men; and when this moral sense is relaxed the guardianship relaxes also. The functional principle does not pretend to be anything but a guide for the practical and political orientation of the moral sense. The English thinkers of the nineteenth century believed they had found a useful orientation for guarding the guardians in the liberal principle. But the liberal principle is not a principle at all, because it does not bind the individual to any kind of solidarity; it leads to incoherence in the societies in which it prevails. It sanctions all desires, legitimate and illegitimate, and all opinions, founded and unfounded. Besides, experience shows that the liberal principle cannot resist the test of a crisis. No war can be fought on liberal principles. At a time of crisis societies are forced to choose between the liberal principle and their preservation—and, though it is possible that a few cranks may prefer the liberal principle, every healthy society will prefer its own preservation. In prefering its own preservation a society abandons itself to the authoritarian principle. This is the story of all modern societies. But in giving itself up to the authoritarian principle a society places itself in hands that will one day strangle it in the dream of a universal monarchy—a fatal result of unlimited authority.

A second argument for the functional principle is to be found in its evident justice. Moral sense tells us that we have a right only to those things which we have paid for in some way, and that the very concept of right can arise only from the consciousness of the services we have rendered. In modern times, in which it has been sought to derive the notion of rights from the subjective concept of personality, and not from services rendered, one speaks of the rights of man or of the rights of woman ; and, above all, of the rights of the child as a crucial example of rights not founded upon services. But this idea is false. The child has no rights. It is his father and society in general who have the duty of bringing him up as an honest man. Right arises only from function. This applies equally to the rights of the individual, the authority, and the State. And that is why the functional principle is superior to the authoritarian and the liberal.

The third argument, of an historical nature, is to be found in the progress of Syndicalism. By Syndicalism I mean the movement which makes men group themselves round the function they fulfil ; not only the workmen, but also the lawyers, doctors, commercial men, and bankers. Against the

Syndicalist theory it has been argued that it deprives man of his rights as a man, acknowledging only those which he possesses as a shoemaker or as a journalist—in short, as a worker. But this argument does not perceive that the functions which a man fulfils are not exhausted with his profession. A man may be at the same time a shoemaker and a soldier and the father of a family, and a member of a co-operative society and a ratepayer in a borough and the citizen of a State ; and he may be associated in different associations for each one of these concepts. In each one of these associations he is a functionary, and he acquires by his function determined rights. The functional principle comprises every possible activity of man and sanctions every one of them with the rights corresponding to the function. The only thing it denies is that a man can acquire rights by the sole fact of his being a man. If the Syndicalist movement progresses in every nation until it embraces practically all men, the day will soon come in which public opinion can see that the syndicates only justify their claims by the function they fulfil. They will not be able to justify them otherwise, for the coal miners cannot found their claims on any other ground than the coal which they produce. In that day the men who do not fulfil functions which the whole of society believes to be necessary will find themselves without any title upon which to base their claims—and not only without titles, but even without the material means of making them effective ; for the only weapon of the syndicates is their possible refusal to render service to society. In this sense society may be afraid of the farmers, the railwaymen, the miners, etc., for it needs food, railways, coal, and so forth. But it need not listen to the claims of the idle rich, thieves, or beggars ; for society does not need either robbery, or beggary, or idleness.

And we must find the fourth reason in the horrors of the present war. Without such a costly and bitter an experience as that of the present war I do not think that men could take upon themselves the labour implied in the organization of human societies on the basis of the functional principle. Nothing is easier than to found a society on liberal principles. It is enough to let men dispute, by every kind of means, positions of social power, provided that they are assured of certain subjective rights by the laws that punish attempts on life or property. Nor is it difficult to found a society on the authoritarian principle. It is enough to entrust the authority with the supreme power over the life, work, and means of the ruled. The functional principle, instead, implies a continual adjustment and readjustment of power to the functions, and of the functions to the values recognized as superior or more urgent. As all men or societies of men will believe themselves to be capable of filling the highest function, and will claim for this function the greatest possible amount of power, it is not to be denied that the functional principle will bring about a permanent struggle, and that only eternal vigilance will prevent this struggle from relapsing into war. More than once the difficulties inherent in the application of the functional principle will cause men to lose heart and fall into the temptation of abandoning themselves to liberal principles and let the individual grasp the position he covets ; or of giving themselves up to authoritarian principles and let a tyrant re-establish order as best he can. But in such moments of dejection the memories of this war will act as a tonic. Men will recall that the liberal principle let loose, in modern centuries, the ambition of individuals, whilst when the liberal principle was corrected by the authoritarian the worst of monsters was unbound : the dream of universal monarchy, the real cause of world-wide wars. And then they will realize that it is worth while going to the trouble of binding the individuals, the authorities, and the nations in the functional principle ; for only thus will it be possible to spare the world the repetition of these horrors.

INDEX

www.ingramcontent.com/pod-product-compliance
Lightning Source LLC
Chambersburg PA
CBHW021615270326
41931CB00008B/710

* 9 7 8 0 6 9 2 0 2 4 6 7 6 *